WITNESS WITHOUT PARALLEL

WITNESS WITHOUT PARALLEL
Eight Biblical Texts
That Make Us Presbyterian

EARL S. JOHNSON, JR.

Geneva Press
Louisville, Kentucky

Grateful acknowledgment is made for excerpts from Thomas John Carlisle, *Beginning with Mary: Women of the Gospels in Portrait,* © 1986 Wm. B. Eerdmans Publishing Company, Grand Rapids, MI. Used by permission; all rights reserved.

Book design by Sharon Adams
Cover design by Lisa Buckley
Cover illustration by Tamara Reynolds

First edition
Published by Geneva Press
Louisville, Kentucky

This book is printed on acid-free paper that meets the American National Standards Institute Z39.48 standard. ∞

PRINTED IN THE UNITED STATES OF AMERICA

05 06 07 08 09 10 11 12 — 10 9 8 7 6 5 4 3 2

Library of Congress Cataloging-in-Publication Data is on file at the Library of Congress, Washington, D.C.

ISBN 0–664–50217–2

To my mother and father,
Elinore and Earl Johnson,
for teaching me what it means
to be Presbyterian

Contents

Preface

The plan for this book was stimulated by some information supplied by my mother and father, church historians at First Presbyterian Church, Williamson, New York. Their research on that congregation's stand in 1818 against slavery sparked a question in my mind about the biblical texts that Presbyterians used to justify that commitment and how their position corresponded with the Reformed theology that was influencing it. This led me to make inquiries about several scriptural passages that motivate us as Presbyterians today and the way current interpretations relate to Presbyterian and Reformed thinking in the past.

Although this study has taken me beyond the areas of research in which I am most knowledgable (i.e., biblical studies and Presbyterian polity), I hope that my attempts to integrate biblical, historical, theological, and practical concepts will be useful for officer training classes, adult education in churches, seminary students learning about biblical interpretation and the way it influences church policy, and discussion and planning groups in higher governing bodies.

I need to give special thanks to Vince Patton of Geneva Press for his guidance and encouragement in the early stages; to David Dobson for guiding me through the final steps of production; to Ella Brazley for careful correction of the early text; to Julie Tonini for work on the final corrections; and to the proofreaders, copyeditors, and other staff at Geneva Press who have aided me so courteously and professionally. I am most grateful to the staffs of the Johnstown Public Library and Swasey Library of Colgate Rochester Divinity School for their cheerful and efficient assistance in my research. I also thank Robert Bullock, editor of *Presbyterian Outlook,* who has given permission to reprint any and all materials already published. My wife, Barbara, has always been patient and supportive when I am writing, even when she wants to see me more and feels compelled to ask, "Are you working on that book again?" I appreciate her encouragement more than words can say.

According to the part of the Constitution of the Presbyterian Church (U.S.A.) first written in 1788, the Holy Scriptures are the only rule of faith and manners for Presbyterians (G-1.0307). One hundred and seventy-nine years later the Confession of 1967 declared that the Scriptures are not a witness among many but a witness without parallel, providing testimony by which the church's faith is nourished and regulated (C-9.27). In this book, I will examine key biblical passages and their relationship to central General Assembly actions (some reaching back to the last quarter of the eighteenth century). Each passage will be considered first in its own original context, in light of its use in Reformed and Presbyterian theology and polity, and then in reference to principles of biblical interpretation used by Christians in the twenty-first century. Throughout I have tried to keep new generations of Presbyterians in mind, believers often not intimately acquainted with these scriptural building blocks, with the hope that they will be helped to understand why the Bible is still important to the church today and how it can be used as ministry prepares for the twenty-first century and beyond.

Introduction

*I*f you were to select passages from the Bible that are the scriptural foundation stones of the Presbyterian Church or the Reformed tradition, which ones would they be?

Discovering the answer to this question is not as easy as it might first appear. Where do you start when you want to describe the biblical basis of Presbyterian faith and polity? What are the scriptural keystones of mission and action in Presbyterian history? Which texts would you choose first and how would you rank them?

Some Presbyterians might think back to their childhood and consider what they were taught in church school or learned in weekly worship. In my church in Williamson, New York, the Ten Commandments were prominently displayed in two separate panels on either side of the pulpit (they still are). Obviously someone thought and still thinks that the word from Mount Sinai is the proper beginning.

But what about other seminal texts in the devotional lives of Christians? Psalm 23 has long been a favorite at Christian funerals and has given believers comfort almost since the time it was written. The two different forms of Jesus' Beatitudes in Matthew 5 and Luke 6 provide critical ethical guidelines for those considering difficult personal and societal decisions. Texts about the resurrection in the Gospels and in 1 Corinthians 15 give us hope; the Christmas narratives in Matthew and Luke provide joy; John 1:1–14 shows us the cosmic purpose of God's incarnation as a human being; 1 Corinthians 12 and 13 instruct us about the nature of the church and the true ways of *agape* love. Should we start with these texts?

Important as these verses are, however, a glance at Presbyterian history might demand a different launch pad. Since the concept of "justification by faith alone" and the appropriate texts in Romans and Galatians were central at the beginning of the Reformation in the minds and hearts of Martin Luther,

John Calvin, and John Knox, it could be argued that they should assume a place of prominence. Or what about other biblical texts that have determined faith and practice in our church or have helped define constitutional principles of freedom of conscience and majority rule in the United States:

- Scriptures at the heart of national crises before the Civil War (how did Presbyterians use passages to argue for slavery and the abolition of slavery at the same time?)
- Verses in Genesis 1 and 2 central in the debate concerning creation and evolution
- Passages prominent in the struggle for civil rights in the middle of the twentieth century

Should scriptural debates involving a wide range of more recent controversies (e.g., the war in Vietnam, women's rights, inclusive language, peace-making in a nuclear age, apartheid, human rights, ecojustice, the ordination of gays and lesbians) also be considered?

If you could decide what these fundamental texts are, what order would you use to discuss them? How could you be sure you had not left out texts that other Presbyterians consider to be essential? Is the quest possible to achieve at all without writing a compendium of Reformed theology or a detailed history of Presbyterian mission?

In the pages that follow, it is assumed that a brief study of selected Bible texts which have served as the basis of Presbyterian faith and action is not only possible but necessary. The starting point of this study will be the basic conviction that Jesus is Lord. Beginning with central faith in Jesus Christ, Christians acknowledge basic commitment to him, and the fundamental knowledge that he is the church's one foundation (1 Cor. 3:11). That Christ stands at the center of our lives and our church is clearly stated in the first page of our Constitution: "All power in heaven and earth is given to Jesus Christ by Almighty God, who raised Christ from the dead and set him above all rule and authority, all power and dominion, and every name that is named, not only in this age but also in that which is to come" (G-1.0100). Despite the current controversy about the historical Jesus and what he truly said and did, we begin with the faith that makes us Christians in the first place and remember the obvious fact that without him there would be no Presbyterian Church at all. In guidelines approved by the General Assembly of the United Presbyterian Church in 1982 for the use of the Bible in Reformed churches, the correct starting point is clearly spelled out: "Recognize that Jesus Christ, the Redeemer, is the center of Scripture."[1]

It is also assumed in these pages that the Bible as a whole is central to our lives as Presbyterians. Despite the fact that we often disagree about the way the Scriptures should be interpreted, all of our debates and important decisions in the past 150 years have been pounded out on the anvil of the Bible.[2] Current discussions are complicated by the fact that scriptural views in the Presbyterian church range all the way from literalistic perspectives asserting that the Bible contains the actual words of God and authoritative historical data throughout, to postmodern constructions that consider the Old and New Testaments to be of no more value than the holy texts of other religious groups or the teaching contained in important secular literature.[3] Yet the Confession of 1967 makes it clear that we have no other place to begin dialogue, since "the Scriptures are not a witness among others, but the witness without parallel. The church has received the books of the Old and New Testaments as prophetic and apostolic testimony in which it hears the Word of God and by which its faith and obedience are nourished and regulated" (C-9.27).

As Presbyterians continue to debate issues of theology and action in the twenty-first century, the Bible will remain central to our discussions, and it will be important to find new ways to discuss differing interpretations without fracturing the body of Christ. Douglas Oldenburg, moderator of the 210th General Assembly (1998), perceptively challenged all Presbyterians to use basic Reformed principles found in the *Book of Confessions* for interpreting the Scriptures and urged every presbytery to hold one-day conferences on the subject of biblical authority to help create new avenues of understanding.[4] Presumably the principles he had in mind include those approved by the General Assembly of the United Presbyterian Church [Northern Church] in 1982:

1. Remember that Jesus Christ is the center of Scripture.
2. Let the focus be on the plain text of Scripture, to the grammatical and historical context, rather than to allegory or subjective fantasy.
3. Depend upon the guidance of the Holy Spirit in interpreting and applying God's message.
4. Be guided by the doctrinal consensus of the church, which is the "rule of faith."
5. Let all interpretations be in accord with the "rule of love"—loving God and loving neighbor.
6. Use earnest study in order to establish the best text, and consider the historical and cultural context in which the message has come. (As the Confession of 1967 expresses it, the Scriptures, given under the guidance of the Holy Spirit, are nevertheless human words, "conditioned by the language, thought forms, and literary fashions of the places and times at which they were written" [C-9.29].)

7. Seek to interpret a particular passage in light of the message of the whole Bible.[5]

A brief examination of recent Presbyterian thinking about the Bible and its authority demonstrates that over the past thirty years we have taken questions about the nature of Scripture and the way it should be used in the church and in the lives of believers very seriously. *Biblical Authority and Interpretation* is an especially useful document for Presbyterians to consider at the advent of the twenty-first century, since it carefully summarizes the history of the discussion in the Reformed tradition in general and in the Presbyterian church in the United States in particular. Correctly observing that "the issue of biblical authority and interpretation is crucial to the life of our denomination because the Scripture has always been considered the one, enduring, trustworthy guide to faith and practice,"[6] the 1982 report also calls Presbyterians to use all the resources of modern biblical criticism (knowledge of Hebrew and Greek, archaeological evidence, textual evidence, cultural, sociological, psychological information, etc.) in order to arrive at the most accurate understanding of biblical texts.[7]

What other guidelines for using the Bible have Presbyterians developed in the past few years? In 1983 the 123rd General Assembly of the Presbyterian Church in the United States [Southern Church] provided a position statement that was similar to the one developed in 1982 by the United Presbyterians. It examined the role of the Bible in the church and utilized many of the same guidelines for the interpretation of texts:

Interpretation . . . usually asks two related kinds of questions. The first asks what the text says and is concerned with understanding its language. The second asks about the use or value of the text for some questions with which one is confronted. . . . The first is that employed in reaching a correct and full understanding of what the texts say. The second is that employed in selecting and using texts for some specific purpose at hand. The first type is composed of the procedures of exegesis; the second is composed of the procedures of theology.[8]

In 1987 the reunited church issued its first extensive statement on the authority of the Bible when the General Assembly of the Presbyterian Church (U.S.A.) approved a document entitled "The Nature of Revelation in the Christian Tradition from a Reformed Perspective."[9] Here revelation is defined as "the self-disclosure of God" that comes primarily through the interaction of the whole person in faith through mind, body, intellect, imagination, emotions, and will with the written word of Scripture and the living Word of Jesus

Christ: "Through God's self-disclosing activity we learn God's purposes and precepts for our lives, God's judgments, and above all God's promises of grace. So understood, revelation is a personal meeting of God with human beings, the experience of which can be reported in language."

Once again the centrality of Christ is emphasized. Even though God does reveal truth through other means (the Old Testament prophets, experience, the action of the Holy Spirit, other religions, etc.),

> to speak of Christ as the central revelation of God is to say . . . that all rev-elation of God must be understood in the light of Christ, and that nothing is to be accepted as revelation that cannot be so understood. All God's deal-ings with humanity form one single story with Jesus at its center. . . . Rev-elation is a continuing process in which God sometimes surprises us with new disclosures of the divine purpose in new situations; but God's revela-tion in Jesus will never be superseded, surpassed, made obsolete, or dis-lodged from its position of centrality.[10]

In "The Nature of Revelation" it is argued that God inspired the authors of the biblical books so that their writings could be used as a vehicle of God's revelation. Although the document does not advocate any particular theory of how this inspiration works, it does make it clear that the Bible is not a text which is simply deposited before us, as if readers were then able to control it simply through the process of interpretation. It requires active involvement—in reading, listening, and acting. The Word, as Heb. 4:12 puts it, is "living and active," and through it we hear "a living voice of God in the Scriptures; and that means that we must turn to them in the expectation that we too will be moved by the Holy Spirit in ways that we could not have predicted."[11]

A fourth document, *Using the Bible: A Guided Study of Presbyterian State-ments on Biblical Authority and Interpretation,* was published by the Theol-ogy and Worship Ministry Unit of the Presbyterian Church (U.S.A.) in 1993, and employs the guidelines approved in 1982 and 1983. *Using the Bible* shows how they can be put to work, and demonstrates how passages should actually be studied by making a careful examination of texts pertaining to questions critical to the church at that time, namely, "marriage and divorce" and "war and peace."[12] Each set of texts is interpreted with two questions in mind—"What do the texts say?" and "How are the texts rightly used?" Pro-viding examples of the way it is possible to overcome the distance between our time and the thoughts and culture of the biblical writers, *Using the Bible* offers a valuable model that can enable churches or groups in presbyteries and synods to develop Bible studies of their own on other texts and topics. The study honestly calls attention to the tensions within the Bible itself about the subjects explored. It urges readers to listen to each other closely in order to arrive at mutual understanding and encourages them to pray together as they seek the Holy Spirit's guidance.[13] It concedes that Bible study undertaken by Presbyterians who may disagree about fundamental principles of scriptural interpretation cannot guarantee that those participating will arrive at identical judgments about the way texts should be interpreted or applied to contemporary Christian life. However, *Using the Bible* demonstrates that such study is still valuable, since it helps provide clarity about the meaning of the text for its first readers and hearers, creates a better understanding of and more tolerance for other people's interpretations of a text, and may lead those taking part to "convergence" in developing some kind of policy or statement that could be useful to the larger body as a whole.[14]

One more study needs to be mentioned to complete an overview of recent Presbyterian perspectives about the Bible. In his 1999 book *Reading the Bible and the Confessions, The Presbyterian Way,* Jack Rogers, moderator of the 213th General Assembly and former professor of theology at San Francisco Theological Seminary, reviews the history of the discussion on the authority of the Bible in the Presbyterian church from its founding through the approval of the Confession of 1967. Rogers employs the seven interpretative guidelines developed in 1982 and 1983, but in his study he is primarily interested in showing how Presbyterians have utilized the Confessions to interpret the Scriptures for their own times and places. In regard to a few selected issues (biblical attitudes toward slavery, puritanical ideas of marriage, essential tenets of the Reformed faith, the role of women, human sexuality), he demonstrates not only what Presbyterians have believed in the past but how the church has changed its mind and has expressed that change in new positions adopted at various meetings of the General Assembly. New interpretations were absolutely necessary, Rogers points out, because in the past theologians and church members imposed theories of biblical inerrancy and the biases of nineteenth-century culture upon their interpretations of the Bible. By reading the mores of their society into the biblical texts, they "lost sight of the fact that the Bible was written in an ancient, Near Eastern culture. And they turned away from the great themes of Scripture: love God and love your neighbor; God makes all things new in Jesus Christ."[15]

In the chapters that follow, several biblical texts will be explored that have been instrumental in forming the basis of Presbyterian belief and stimulating Presbyterian life and mission. By using Reformed and Presbyterian principles of scriptural interpretation and modern biblical criticism to examine theological statements and positions on social issues taken by the Presbyterian church throughout its history, I hope that we will do more than merely rediscover the actual texts that form the scriptural building blocks of faith and action. Perhaps we can also understand and avoid interpretative mistakes of the past and provide insights into the way the Bible can be used correctly to lead the church in the future. As Rogers puts it, by examining the mistakes of our forebears, we may discover new ways to use the Bible (and the Confessions) as helps rather than rules, and find the courage to try, as those before us tried, to apply Christ's message to our own time and context.[16]

In the studies that follow, scriptural passages will not be listed as mere proof texts, as if that method alone would provide positive results. Although in the past Presbyterians have used proof-texting (the piling up of Bible verses to demonstrate that a proposition is true) to develop faith positions, such an approach conflicts with the principles of modern biblical criticism by taking passages out of context and ignoring cultural and historical backgrounds. More often than not this has led to a misunderstanding of God's will, not an affirmation of the love of God in Christ.[17] Here texts have not been chosen as subject headings because they have some ineffable authority and power in and of themselves or provide the sole argument for a particular point of view, but because they have served (or may serve) as traditional focal points around which clusters of texts orbit, demonstrating how several passages illustrate God's will and provide similar descriptions of human behavior. Texts have been chosen to illustrate themes and concepts because they provide theological hooks—words and concepts easily remembered—on which we may hang our faith and a solid scriptural rationale for our actions.

There is a final reason why an appreciation of how the Bible has been used in the past is necessary for a correct self-understanding as Presbyterians. Over thirty years ago, James D. Smart warned about the growing silence of the Bible in the church. In his view the Bible was failing to maintain its place in the lives of congregations and denominations and in the lives of individual Christians.[18] Since he sounded his alarm, Presbyterians have continued to hold Bible classes, preach scriptural sermons, develop a new catechism, and train pastors and other church leaders in biblical criticism, but the danger still exists that the biblical basis of our faith and action may erode further. A Christian education survey conducted by the Search Institute in 1990 revealed that only 34 percent of Protestants in the United States devote time to reading and studying the Bible.[19] The survey, which developed a definition of "mature faith" that incorporated thirty-eight different elements, also concluded that although nearly all mainline adults embody some of the elements, the areas that are most problematic are those having to do directly with spiritual growth and action: Bible reading and prayer, talking with others about one's faith, involvement in the pursuit of social justice, and so forth. Furthermore 38 percent of Protestant adults have what is called "undeveloped faith" or "a lack of faith maturity."[20] By calling attention to the texts that made (and make) us who we are, I hope that those already grounded in the Scriptures will be reminded why they are Presbyterians. By introducing Bible passages central to Presbyterian identity to new generations of church leaders, a tool will be provided to help them understand why the Bible is important in the church and will continue to be in the future.

A word about organization: In each chapter, keeping in mind the guidelines for Bible study that have been developed by the Presbyterian Church in the past twenty or more years, five different perspectives will be used to enable the study of the texts that have helped Presbyterians become who they are.

The centrality of the text. Each chapter will introduce the significance of the biblical text (or texts) in the Bible and its importance for Presbyterians.

The text. This section will provide a brief overview of the background of the text (or texts), why it was written, how the particular passage and its vocabulary were influenced by the situation, culture, and thought-forms of the author (or authors), and how the passage relates to clusters of passages elsewhere in the Bible that have similar emphases.

Use in the Reformed tradition and the Presbyterian Church. The third section will make a more detailed review of the way in which the text (or texts) impacted Reformed theology and practice and how the text has been interpreted in the Presbyterian church.

Prospects—How can the text be rightly used in the future? "Do your best to present yourself to God as one approved . . . , rightly explaining the word of truth" (2 Tim. 2:15). Here questions will be asked about how the text is understood in the church today and how it is likely to be interpreted in the future. Will this text be important to Presbyterians in the years to come? If so, how will it influence our discussions and debates and how will its interpretation mold our decisions about theology and mission?

Questions for study. In the final section, questions will be provided to enable discussion groups to engage in further dialogue and study.

Chapter 1

Jesus Is Lord

Romans 10:9

If you confess with your lips that Jesus is Lord and believe in your heart that God raised him from the dead, you will be saved.

Centrality of the Text

*T*he profession that Jesus is Lord is the starting point of faith for the individual Christian and for the church as a whole. If anyone asks what the fundamental criterion of being a Christian is, it is only necessary to cite Rom. 10:9.

In the Presbyterian Church it is this basic belief that forms the foundation stone for membership and ordination. When new members join the church they are asked one of two questions:

- Do you turn to Jesus Christ and accept him as your Lord and Savior, trusting in his grace and love?

or

- Who is your Lord and Savior? (to which the answer is, "Jesus Christ is my Lord and Savior")

Likewise when pastors, elders, or deacons are ordained, they are asked,

- Do you trust in Jesus Christ your Savior, acknowledge him Lord of all and Head of the Church, and through him believe in one God, Father, Son, and Holy Spirit? Will you in your own life seek to follow the Lord Jesus Christ, love your neighbors, and work for the reconciliation of the world? (cf. G-14.0207)

At the end of the ordination service, the moderator cites words from Col. 3:17 as a final blessing to orient the ministry about to begin: "Whatever you do, in word or deed, do everything in the name of the Lord Jesus" (G-14.0209).

Presbyterians know where their starting point is and who it is that stands at the center of faith.

The Text

The New Testament word "Lord" (*kurios* in Greek) essentially has to do with the worlds of business and government and is a title for landowners, employers, slave masters, political officials, and rulers. It is an expression of respect, and its fundamental meaning is "master, boss, sir" and is used that way a number of times in Jesus' teaching (Luke 19:11–27; Matt. 6:24; 21:40; 25:14–30; Mark 12:1–12). In some passages it refers to the belief prevalent in the first century in gods, goddesses, powers, and authorities who were also called *kurioi* or *kuria* (plural, 1 Cor. 8:5–6). In Rom. 10:9, and in the majority of New Testament texts, *kurios* is elevated to a title of honor reserved for Jesus Christ as the Son of God, the Lord who saves God's children from sin, and one who is worthy of the highest praise and worship. Paul uses it over two hundred times in this way, and it is clear that there was a wide consensus among early Christians that Jesus deserved much more than secular respect and honor: He is the risen and glorified Christ who existed with God from the beginning (see, for example, John 1:1–14; Col. 1:15–20; Heb. 1:1–4).[1] Since the title *kurios* was frequently used in descriptions of the Roman emperor or in prayers to him, it is very likely that Paul draws a sharp contrast between the allegiance of Roman citizens and the faith of Christians in Jesus Christ. The true Lord of the world, Paul asserts, is not any imperial personage, no matter how much power he has. It is the Lord Jesus Christ, who is the ruler of all.[2]

Paul often uses the title "Lord" in conjunction with Old Testament texts to demonstrate that Jesus has the same name of honor and identical power with God. Although Joel 2:32, cited in Rom. 10:13, refers to God in the original text, Paul uses it to reiterate his strong conviction that Jesus Christ as Lord is the one who dissolves all distinctions between Jews and Greeks: "For, 'Everyone who calls on the name of the Lord shall be saved.'" In the Greek version of the Old Testament (Septuagint), the word *kurios* is repeatedly used to translate Hebrew words for the name of God. In Rom. 10, Paul makes a clear Trinitarian statement by indicating that the God referred to by the prophet Joel is one and the same with Jesus Christ.[3] In other texts he goes further and says that Jesus not only has the name of God but is equal to God. In the hymn to Christ found in Phil. 2:1–11, for example, he writes,

> Therefore God also highly exalted him
>   and gave him the name
>   that is above every name,
> so that at the name of Jesus
>   every knee should bend,
>   in heaven and on earth and under the earth,
>   and every tongue should confess
>   that Jesus Christ is Lord,
>   to the glory of God the Father.[4]

In Rom. 10, Paul also indicates the particular way in which Jesus' Lordship causes him to stand at the center of the church's confession, (i.e., through the resurrection). In Paul's view, there is no way to be a Christian without commitment to Jesus as Lord, because his Lordship is intimately involved with his power and presence as the one who is raised from the dead. You must do more than think that he was a great man, an incisive teacher, or one inspired by the divine, Paul implies. Nothing is said here about the nature of Jesus' birth, his miracles, the authority of his teachings, or his demands for discipleship. Rather, the central affirmation is a simple one: If you believe in your heart that God raised him from the dead, you will be saved.

The fundamental criterion for being a Christian is believing that Jesus is the Lord who lives. One cannot pretend to be a Christian while rejecting the resurrection. Paul restates this principle without equivocation in 1 Cor. 15:17–20: "If Christ has not been raised, your faith is futile and you are still in your sins. Then those also who have died in Christ have perished. If for this life only we have hoped in Christ, we are of all people most to be pitied. But in fact Christ has been raised from the dead, the first fruits of those who have died." As Joseph Fitzmyer says about Rom. 10,

> Paul thus introduces his fundamental assertion about Christian faith. . . .
> This is not a mere external or public affirmation, but the inmost and profound dedication of a person to God in the Lord Jesus. What Paul acknowledges here has become the affirmation par excellence of Christian faith.[5]

As 1 Cor. 16:22 and Rev. 22:20 indicate, the first believers did not stop at the resurrection but went a step further. Christians extended faith in Jesus as Lord beyond recognition of the fact that he was the risen Christ to the confidence that he would come again at the time of God's judgment. Using the Aramaic expression *marana tha,* "our Lord, come," they expressed their belief that Jesus would come one more time. Although some biblical scholars have doubted that the use of the Aramaic in this expression has any historical

Jewish roots (they assume that the early church created it out of pagan religious concepts), evidence from the Dead Sea Scrolls demonstrates that Jews writing prior to the time of the composition of the New Testament texts did refer to God as "my Lord" and "our Lord."[6] Fragments of texts from *1 Enoch* found in Qumran Cave 4 (written from the end of the third century B.C. to the beginning of the first century A.D.) indicate that the use of *kurios* to express Jesus' transcendent divine power definitely found its origin in Palestinian-Semitic roots and was not something made up by the first Christians merely to generate a stronger case among Gentile listeners.[7]

Beyond the usage of the title "Lord" in such an exalted sense, there is a related but seemingly disconnected application in which addressing Jesus as Lord moves past ethereal and eternal realms to one much closer to home, to the concepts of intimacy and absolute trust. For the first believers, Jesus was more than their master, the head of the church, and the Lord of the universe. He was also someone they knew and loved, one who could be called "my Lord" in a reverential and personal manner. In such cases, Jesus received prayers and statements of confidence that would normally have been reserved for a spouse or close friend. Paul speaks from the heart, for example, about living and dying to the Lord (Rom. 14:8), of undivided loyalty to him (1 Cor. 7:35), of personal visions and revelations the Lord has given him (2 Cor. 12:1), about begging him to take away his suffering (2 Cor. 12:8). For Christian believers, Jesus is more than the unique Son of God raised to power by God; he is also one who cares about us and gives us the most individual kind of attention.

Use in the Reformed Tradition and the Presbyterian Church

In 1993, on the tenth anniversary of the reunification of the northern and southern streams of the Presbyterian church, the 205th General Assembly approved a statement that reaffirms the central significance of belief in Jesus as Lord in the Reformed tradition:

> The church is called to bear witness to God's saving work in Jesus Christ, the Word made flesh who has come among us full of grace and truth (John 1:14; Acts 1:8). The church seeks to live Christ's teachings and to be governed by him as Lord of the church, and Savior of the world. . . . The Word of God incarnate in Jesus of Nazareth and written in the Old Testament (the Hebrew Scriptures) and the New Testament are authoritative for our understanding of the nature of the church. The Presbyterian Form of Government is based on our interpretation of these Scriptures.[8]

This fundamental principle can easily be traced back to the writings of the Reformers, especially in their commentaries. In regard to Gal. 1:3, for example, Luther asks why Paul extends grace "from God our Father and the Lord Jesus Christ"? Would it not be enough merely to mention God? Luther answers in the negative because we need to know that "there is no other God besides this man Jesus Christ." The fact that Jesus as Lord and God as Father are one is demonstrated clearly in his incarnation. If you have any trouble understanding salvation, he writes, run straight to the manger and to the Virgin's little babe in arms. See him as he was born, growing up, teaching, dying, and rising again, and you will be able to shake off all terrors and errors, knowing that Christ is very God.[9] More simply, John Calvin, commenting on 1 Cor. 12:3, writes that no one can praise Christ without the Spirit: "To say that Jesus is Lord means to speak of Him with honour and reverence, and to extol His majesty."[10]

In the Presbyterian Church (U.S.A.), the Form of Government begins with the assertion that all things are under the Lordship of Jesus Christ (G-1.0100a). By affirming with the earliest Christians that Jesus is Lord, we confess that he is our hope and that we are free to live in the lively, joyous reality of the grace of God (G-1.0100d). In the local (particular) church, one becomes a member through faith in Jesus Christ and acceptance of his Lordship in all of life (G-5.0101; 4.0103). What is more, all Christians come to God in the same way, since the church universal consists of all persons in every nation who profess faith in Jesus Christ as Lord and Savior and commit themselves to live in a fellowship under his rule (G-4.0101).[11]

Indeed, from the beginning, the church catholic has insisted that confession of Jesus as Lord is an essential component of Trinitarian conviction. The assertion in the second paragraph of the Apostles' Creed can be traced to early New Testament creedal statements (C-2.2). The insistence in the Nicene Creed that the church believes "in one Lord Jesus Christ, the only-begotten Son of God" (C-1.2) reflects the battle with Arianism and with those who stated that Jesus was not really the same as God, but only like God.[12] The 198th General Assembly (1986) explained why belief in the Trinity is important to modern Christians:

At the heart of all confessions is the earliest confession of the New Testament church, "Jesus is Lord." (Strictly speaking, therefore, Christians confess not what but in whom they believe.) But the church discovered very early that in order to protect this simple confession from misunderstanding and misuse, it had to talk about the relation between Jesus and the God of Israel, and between Jesus and the Holy Spirit. The earliest Christological Confession became a Trinitarian confession. . . . Moreover, the church could not talk about the "lordship" of Jesus without also talking about the claim the triune God has on the lives of people in their personal and social relationships in the church and in the world.[13]

The 213th General Assembly (2001) reaffirmed this fundamental commitment by voting 369–163 to confess "the unique authority of Jesus as Lord" and refer to Jesus Christ as "uniquely Savior." While acknowledging that Presbyterians do not know the limits of God's grace for those who are not Christians, the assembly affirmed, "The transforming power of Christ in our lives compels us to make Christ known to others." At the next General Assembly (2002), commissioners overwhelmingly approved a statement entitled "Hope in the Lord Jesus Christ" that calls all people everywhere to place their faith, love, and hope in him.

Thus, it is not surprising that in most recent confessions the concept of the Lordship of Jesus was a key component in critical political decisions the church was compelled to make. In the Theological Declaration of Barmen, representatives of all the German Confessional Churches met in 1934 to confess the one Lord of the holy, apostolic church (C-8.01; 8.06) and to boldly denounce the claims of Hitler. Making it clear that they had no Führer other than Jesus Christ, they wrote: "Through him befalls us a joyful deliverance from the godless fetters of this world for a free, grateful service to his creatures. We reject the false doctrine, as though there were areas of our life in which we would not belong to Jesus Christ, but to other lords" (C-8.14–15). The Confession of 1967 reflected the struggles in the United States concerning issues of civil rights and the Vietnam War when Presbyterians declared that Jesus is the ground of the peace, justice, and freedom among nations that all powers of government are called to serve and defend. As nations continue to develop weapons of mass destruction, the Confession proclaims, they must understand that they are to do more than serve their own people; they are responsible to Jesus Christ. Likewise, the church must not make the mistake of associating the gospel with the policies of a nation or a particular political party: "Although nations may serve God's purposes in history, the church which identifies the sovereignty of any one nation or any one way of life with the cause of God denies the Lordship of Christ and betrays its calling" (C-9.45).

Prospects: How Can the Text Be Rightly Used in the Future?

As we look ahead in our denomination, what significance will our profession of Jesus as Lord be likely to have? What commitments will we need to make in mission and evangelism? What questions will we need to raise to make growth (and survival) possible?

Certainly there should be little doubt that the Presbyterian Church will continue to be dedicated to worldwide mission. We will not need to be reminded that the risen Lord has called us to witness to all of the nations of the world in his name (Matt. 28:16–20). As churches continue to grow at exponential rates in many areas of Africa, Asia, and Central and South America, Presbyterians will need to renew the basic conviction that ours is a body "called to be a sign in and for the world of the new reality which God has made available to people in Jesus Christ" (G-3.0200). We only need to remember what we have already committed ourselves to doing: to invite those of "every tribe, tongue, people, and nation" to join us in turning to the living God by following the example of Christ, and to bring the good news to those suffering from the guilt of sin, those controlled by dehumanizing forces, those who are enduring physical suffering or mental anguish, those who feel deserted, homeless, or orphaned, those who are caught in the trap of materialism and pleasure, those struggling against injustice, oppression, evil institutions, structures, and persons.[14]

In my own travels I have seen what Presbyterians are already doing in places such as Nicaragua, Mexico, Israel, and various parts of Africa. What we have accomplished in Jesus' name is stunning. What remains yet to be done is nearly overwhelming. And we can remember that mission in other countries is not entirely dependent on professionals hired by the General Assembly. (It is difficult to thank them enough for their sacrificial ministries.) Congregations can raise money and send pastors and lay leaders to help rebuild church buildings, provide medical assistance, and teach and preach for short periods of time through the International Volunteer Office.[15] One church I served as pastor has been sending volunteers for years to places such as Ethiopia, Sudan, Mozambique, and Brazil to assist with mission projects endorsed by the General Assembly. Most recently, my current congregation raised money as part of a capital fund drive to sponsor three of us to work with S.E.R.V.E.[16] to help rebuild a church in Mabilibile, Mozambique, that had been destroyed by the civil war in 1992. In regard to these projects, it is hard to say who is the most excited by Christ's service or benefits the most: those whose ministries are strengthened or those who respond to Christ's call to be partners in mission with brothers and sisters across the world.

Ironically, as beneficial as it is to engage in witness in other countries, it is becoming increasingly clear to many Presbyterians that much of our mission in the future will not require trips abroad but may come about without volunteers ever leaving their own towns and cities. In the northeastern United

States, for example, numerous congregations have become primary mission fields themselves. Their communities have suffered severe economic setbacks. Industries have moved or closed, former manufacturing sites present eyesores and/or environmental hazards, waste sites need to be cleaned up at enormous costs, employment is down, and people are discouraged about dwindling worship attendance in local congregations. In declining areas young people have moved away, and many of our neighbors do not seem to be interested in the church or its mission.

What we may not yet see is that rather than confronting us with an intractable problem, God may be laying before us a great opportunity that has not yet found a solution. If the secular culture causes some people to be neutral, or even hostile, toward the gospel, we may find ourselves in a situation very similar to the one Jesus and the disciples knew when the church was just beginning. To rebuild the kingdom and grow the church, we may have to rely on the Holy Spirit more, realizing again that we cannot do it alone. We may need to pray more intently and return to a primary message that promises people a new way to live and brings God's healing to those who are so busy that they do not even realize they are bruised and diseased. It is possible that we will have to cooperate with churches in other denominations more intentionally as we realize that we can accomplish more if congregations share ministry and work together instead of attempting to do everything alone at increasingly high costs.

If the Presbyterian Church continues to lose members every year and we can only bring new people into the church one at a time in some communities, we should thank God that we are in good company, since Jesus also spent so much of his time ministering to individuals. If it is difficult to attract teenagers or young parents to the church, we may realize that this job calls for the most creative ideas we have, and the maximum of energy and enthusiasm.

Now is not the time to become discouraged because we seem to be in decline in some parts of the country. Instead, we can be glad that we have been entrusted with such a challenging opportunity and that we are forced to depend on One who is more powerful than we, that God is recalling us to basic mission work again, and that in the future, going into all the world will also mean going down our own street and up our own lane if our denomination is to survive.

What is more, new opportunities to witness to Christ present themselves all the time if we are willing to see changing religious perspectives as possibilities rather than threats. In the last few years, for example, interest in the person and work of Jesus has reached an unprecedented level, stimulated initially by the reports of the so-called Jesus Seminar, a group of biblical scholars convened to determine the exact words of Jesus.[17] As a result, weekly magazines,[18] reports on PBS, and made-for-television movies[19] have repeatedly explored fundamental questions about Jesus' personality and mission. Many Americans appear to be fascinated by the theories biblical scholars propose. Who was Jesus really—a simple peasant teaching homespun truths, a sophisticated philosopher formed in the Cynic mold, an apocalyptic visionary who expected the end at any moment, or a revolutionary leader calling God's people to resist the oppression of the religious and political elite in order to foster a kingdom in which God's declaration of jubilee would truly be realized? In the years to come, it is possible that this increased discussion about Jesus may present Christians with exciting opportunities for evangelism, church growth, and Christian education, as millions of Americans continue to be vitally interested in his true identity and what his genuine teachings really signify for daily living.

One critical caveat is in order. If recent debates within the Presbyterian Church (U.S.A.) about Jesus' identity are any indication, it is not difficult to see how we could miss the opportunities being presented to us for work, witness, and education. A church fractured by fundamental disagreement, mistrust, and rancor runs the risk of having its message become ineffectual, as people we try to reach wonder why they should become part of any organization that is obviously divided by factionalism and party spirit. The disturbing division of our denomination into theological camps will not make it more inviting to outsiders. It may cause them to wonder if we really think that Jesus is also divided (1 Cor. 1:13).[20]

A major case in point involves the recent heated discussion that followed the presentation made by the Rev. Dirk Ficca at the 2000 Peacemaking Conference at Chapman University, Orange, California. In an address entitled "Uncommon Ground: Living Faithfully in a Diverse World,"[21] Ficca, an ordained Presbyterian pastor and the executive director of the Parliament of the World's Religions in Chicago, spoke out of his own experience of interacting with people from many faith traditions. Drawing a distinction between talking about differences between religions (beliefs and practices) and the fundamental factors that create a religion's identity, he suggested that Christians can maintain integrity without trying to proselytize those who do not believe in Jesus Christ. In answer to the question "How can a Christian live out his or her own particular faith while being fully engaged in a religiously pluralistic world?" Ficca put forth a theological perspective that takes away the offensiveness of evangelistic efforts often perceived in an interfaith environment. If we take the *instrumental* view, Ficca argues, that salvation only comes through Jesus, dialogue is effectively cut off. But if we take what can be called a *revelatory* view, it can be said that salvation comes primarily through God's Spirit. If it is God who saves us, then although it is correct to profess that Jesus saves, a pluralist view can also be affirmed that God works in other places and in other ways to reconcile the world.

The response to Ficca's presentation was negative and swift. Twenty-one sessions of the Presbyterian Church (U.S.A.) and one presbytery asked the General Assembly to discipline him or require him to deny the views he had expressed. Presbyterian chat rooms on the Internet were flooded with comments that claimed such opinions to be "heretical," "false teaching," "the demotion of Jesus."[22] The executive director of the General Assembly Council, John Detterick, told a meeting of the Presbyterian Coalition that the speech conflicted with a basic tenet of the church's faith and was "out of bounds." Later, the General Assembly Council issued a longer statement saying that although it does not have the authority to make theological statements on behalf of the church or take judicial action against speakers, the Council affirmed the basic concept of "the Lordship of Jesus Christ and our salvation through Christ." At the same time, it commended the Peacemaking Program for sponsoring open dialogue and attempting to explore emerging perspectives at its conferences.[23] The reaffirmation of the Lordship of Jesus Christ as Lord and Savior by the 213th General Assembly (2001) was, in large part, a response to this controversy. Later that year the General Assembly Council endorsed a statement written by the Office of Theology and Worship that reiterates the basic Presbyterian belief, found in the *Book of Confessions,* that faith in "Jesus as Lord" is foundational. This Presbyterian commitment was further confirmed in 2002.

After some time has passed, one can hope that it will be possible to make more objective responses. In light of the church's affirmations about Jesus as Lord and the centrality of the doctrine of justification by faith alone (see the discussion in chapter 2), it is easy to grasp why Ficca's comments drew such fiery reactions. Although those who work with people from other faiths understand the sensitivity that is required if open dialogue is to continue, it is not necessary to jettison the heart of Reformed theology to have ongoing discussion. In these settings, whether it is in the context of faith discussion or in worship, it is possible to maintain one's core beliefs and state them clearly without adopting a position that conflicts with New Testament definitions and the central statements of Presbyterian polity and doctrine. Alternative approaches do exist. As the 203rd General Assembly proposed, citing an earlier report of the World Council of Churches, our witness to people of other religions does not have to be offensive to remain in keeping with the Reformed tradition.

The spirit that is to inform our witness among people of other faiths ". . . presupposes our presence with them, sensitivity to their deepest faith commitments and experiences, willingness to be their servants for Christ's sake, affirmation of what God has done and is doing among them and love for them." As Christians our faith demands that we seek to build loving relationships with persons of other faiths. Where possible we will work with them in struggles for justice, freedom, peace, and human dignity.[24]

The 211th General Assembly (1999) provides numerous suggestions in a plan for study and action entitled *Building Community among Strangers.*[25]

Nevertheless, care must be taken to avoid a kind of "knee-jerk" theology (which often develops in situations where groups feel that they are being discounted or unheard) in which it is assumed that a duty exists to look for heresy everywhere unorthodox language is used, especially in open forums meant to stimulate thought. Basic questions need to be asked about being Presbyterian together. If honest inquiries cannot be presented at a peacemaking conference about how we are to get along with people with whom we have radical spiritual differences, where can they be raised? In our membership and ordination vows, have we committed ourselves to the rule that contrary views will never be expressed at official PC(USA) gatherings? When is the appropriate time to raise theological questions of the most fundamental nature? When can speakers play devil's advocate or express opinions that may not represent a majority perspective?

In the local church the same issues must be faced. What does the pastor or session do when members express questions about the Reformed tradition, or wonder openly about christological statements found in the *Book of Confessions* or in the *Constitution*? Should they be excluded from membership or ordination because their beliefs are not in the majority? Should surprising or unorthodox questions create the paranoid fear that heresy may take root in our congregations, or can they present refreshing opportunities for dialogue and education?

In the new century, the increasingly pluralistic culture in which we live will make it necessary to rethink the content of our witness and our responses to questions about Jesus' identity that are raised by neighbors who do not have a Reformed or biblical background. How we do that may test our faithfulness to the One who commanded us to witness to them and be in dialogue with them in the first place.[26] As the 189th General Assembly stated it,

> In every time and place the church is called to make the implications of its fundamental confession of the Lordship of Jesus Christ unmistakably clear and relevant. But in order to do that it has had in every new situation to decide afresh what to say and what to leave unsaid, how much and how little to say, what to emphasize and what for the time being to pass over, which internal and external dangers are critical and which are less critical.[27]

Questions for Study and Reflection

1. In your own thinking, what does it mean to say that Jesus is "the way, the truth, and the life" (John 14:6)? In what sense is he the only way for you to salvation? Do you think that he is also the only way for people of other faiths? How is that true if they have never heard of Jesus?
2. When you say that Jesus Christ is your Lord and Savior, what does that mean to you personally? When you think of Jesus as Lord, do you picture him as a powerful person who has authority over you, or someone who is close and loves you? Or are both images valid at once?
3. How do you think the concept of Jesus as Lord should be discussed in our denomination? How central will that affirmation be in the future?
4. Read over the various descriptions of Jesus in the historic confessions in the *Book of Confessions.* Which one is most meaningful to you? Which one will be the most important to the church in the future?

Chapter 2

Justification by Faith Alone

Romans 1:16–17 and 3:26

For I am not ashamed of the gospel; it is the power of God for salvation to everyone who has faith, to the Jew first and also to the Greek. For in it the righteousness of God is revealed through faith for faith; as it is written, 'The one who is righteous will live by faith.'

Centrality of the Text

*T*he doctrine of justification by faith alone has been a key concept since the beginning of the Christian church. Repeatedly, new understandings of its ramifications for faith and action have created critical moments of discovery for those who faced crises in the church's growth and development. For Paul, it provided a key to his struggle to keep the Ten Commandments and the rest of the Jewish law while at the same time entering the freedom of the Christian life. Discovering that God saves us from our sin, not by what we do but only through our faith in what God gives, was a spiritual breakthrough of gigantic proportions for him.

In the sixteenth century, the texts of Rom. 1:16–17; 3:21–31; 4:14, 24–25; and Gal. 2:15–21 resolved a crisis of faith for Martin Luther as well. Luther's preaching on the concept of justification by faith opened his eyes to the spiritual abuses of the Roman Catholic Church of his time, especially the sale of indulgences, documents which indicated that sin had been forgiven. In the year before his death, Luther wrote that Paul's teaching in Rom. 1:16–17 gave him a new life: "Here I felt that I was altogether born again and had entered paradise itself through open gates. There a totally other face of the entire Scripture showed itself to me."[1] Somewhat less dramatically, John Calvin refers to the same text as "the main hinge on which religion turns": "For unless you first of all grasp what your relationship to God is, and the nature of his [*sic*] judgment concerning you, you have neither a foundation on which to establish your salvation nor one on which to build piety toward God."[2]

More than 380 years later, the German theologian Karl Barth turned to Romans in another moment of crisis. Publishing the first edition of his commentary on Romans just one month after the end of World War I, Barth, thirty years old, already sensed that history was "between the times" and that a new generation of Christians needed a renewed understanding of the relationship between law and gospel, or, as he liked to order it, "gospel and law," since he thought that God's grace should always come first, the love of God being aimed at bringing our actions into conformity with God's own.[3] In Romans he found "something quite surprising and strange": "It was often as though I caught a breath from afar . . . something primeval . . . indefinably sunny, wild, original, that somehow is hidden behind these sentences."[4]

The Text

The key texts are Rom. 1:16–17 and 3:21–26. In the first passage, Paul uses a modified version of Hab. 2:4 to set the stage for the rest of the letter and for his theology as a whole.[5] Although commentators disagree when pressed to discover the most important reason for the writing of Romans, it would appear, as A. J. M. Wedderburn puts it, that there is a cluster of interlocking factors that explain its composition.[6] Among them are:

- the debate between Jewish Christians and "law-free" believers who sharply disagree about the value of the Jewish law for salvation;
- the present situation in Rome and Paul's desire to make a strong statement (possibly a political one) to the imperial powers;[7]
- the significance of his own future goals, especially the impending trip to Jerusalem to relieve the situation of some churches in the midst of an economic downturn (Acts 15:25–27), his desired missionary tour to Spain (15:24, 28), and a possible journey to the church in Rome itself (15:29).[8]

In Romans, Paul struggles with the concept found in some Old Testament texts that one is forgiven by God only by adhering to strict legal requirements through the keeping of all the law and traditional interpretations of it (cf. Deut. 27:1; 28:1, 15; Ps. 119:1–8; Mark 7:1–23). Realizing that believers are lost if salvation depends upon perfect adherence to the law or a system of ritual sacrifice in its name, since it is impossible to achieve the perfection that God ultimately requires, Paul discovers that a right relationship with God is only possible through the free gift (grace) given in the death and resurrection of Jesus Christ.

"Justification," in the expression "justification by faith," comes from the Greek word *dikaioō* and the Hebrew *sdq,* and other words related to the same verbal roots, and together they occur about 750 times in the Bible.[9] Although justification can take on a legal or forensic meaning, indicating an act that acquits or pardons a person for a crime, in Romans it also has a personal tone—the action in Christ by which human beings are restored to a right relationship with God, one previously broken by sin.[10] C. H. Dodd demonstrates that in regard to justification God can take on the role of a judge (pardoning for a crime, Rom. 8:1), an emancipator (freeing the oppressed from slavery, Rom. 5:15–17; Gal. 4:7; 5:1), or a priest (performing acts that will allow the sinner to be forgiven through a blood sacrifice, Rom. 3:25, 5:15–16; Gal. 5:1): "from condemnation to acquittal, from bondage to freedom, from guilt to innocence."[11] In all three instances, God changes the status of the believer through a free gift of grace and love. For Paul, a believer becomes "righteous," that is, is made right with God, is acquitted, or is freed from sin, through faith in Jesus Christ and his death on the cross.

What is this faith that makes justification possible? In Hebrew thought, the core concept is of firmness, reliability, steadfastness: "To believe is to hold on to something firmly, with conviction and confidence."[12] In Paul's writings, as Ernest Best points out, it is almost easier to say what faith *is not* than what it *is*.[13] For Paul, it is not simply a system of belief, it is not an emotional feeling, it is not a faithfulness to a system or organization. Instead, it is the attitude in people that is called out by the way in which God has given the Son to save humanity. It is the attitude in people awakened when they see what God has done for them. It is openness to God and a recognition that all is a gift; striving after rewards and yearning for recognition from God are no longer necessary.[14] All we need has already been given.

Although the word "alone" in the expression "justification by faith alone" does not appear anywhere in Paul's writings, it does not misrepresent his thinking substantially. For him, there is no other way to be reconciled to God except through the grace brought about by Jesus' death and resurrection: "For God has done what the law, weakened by the flesh, could not do": by sending the Son in the likeness of sinful flesh, God condemned sin (Rom. 8:3).[15] It is only through Christ's sacrifice and our faith in him that we can be saved (Rom. 5:1).

In Rom. 4, Paul gives the clinching argument when he looks at the story of Abraham. Since Abraham was the one in whom God began blessing the people of Israel (Gen. 12:1–5; 17:5), Paul is able to show that Abraham was saved not by his actions (leaving his home in Ur [Gen. 12:1–3], or nearly sacrificing his only son, Isaac [Gen. 22]), but in his faith in God. Abraham's faith, not his works, was "reckoned to him as righteousness" (Rom. 4:23). His story becomes a living example for Paul and his readers through their faith in Jesus: "Now the words, 'it was reckoned to him,' were written not for his sake alone, but for ours also. It will be reckoned to us who believe in him who raised Jesus our Lord from the dead, who was handed over to death for our trespasses and was raised for our justification"(4:23–25; see Gal. 3:6–4:31).

Focus on the importance of justification by faith is not limited, of course, only to texts found in Romans. It is a theme that runs through many of Paul's major writings. In Galatians it stands at the center of his defense of his own apostleship.[16] Peter's inconsistent attempt to side with those who believe in freedom from the law at one time, and his desire to team up with Judaizers at another (Gal. 2:11–14), angers and disgusts Paul. As he forcefully asserts in Gal. 2:16: "We know that a person is justified not by the works of the law but through faith in Jesus Christ. And we have come to believe in Christ Jesus, so that we might be justified by faith in Christ, and not by doing the works of the law, because no one will be justified by the works of the law." Those who want to be justified by the law have cut themselves off from Christ and have fallen away from the free gift of love in God (5:4). By contrast, those who rely on faith "eagerly wait for the hope of righteousness" (5:5). The theme of justification by faith is also clearly in mind in other writings in which Paul particularly links it with Jesus' resurrection and the threefold connection of faith, hope, and love (see 1 Thess. 1:3, 8; 4:14; 5:8; 1 Cor. 13:13; 2 Cor. 4:14–16; Phil. 1:27).[17]

The problem of justification Paul struggles with throughout Romans and Galatians is misunderstood if one assumes that he despaired because he initially thought he was not good enough to stand before God. Actually, the opposite was probably the case. As a Pharisee who had studied the law in the minutest detail, Paul was of the opinion that he had kept the law perfectly. As he says in Phil. 3:6, his struggle with his faith did not result from a lack of self-esteem; more likely, he was probably so sure of himself and what he could do that not even God could penetrate his shield of self-confidence.

The big surprise for Paul was that once he became a Christian he realized that nothing he did was good enough to earn him God's favor. As he says in Phil. 3:7, Christ was showing him that what he once thought was valuable is actually worthless. What could he do, after all, that would impress the Creator of the universe? And how could he be so naive to think that he could achieve perfection? Once he realized how great God is in Christ, he understood how unimpressive his own ability to keep the law really was. What is more, he then began to learn that at that point it ceased to matter any more. Once you understand who Jesus Christ is, you have also accepted the fact that he has rescued you from sin, and the whole discussion ultimately becomes pointless. Your faith in Christ is what has saved you, not what you do or say, so all one can do is respond in praise and thanks: "Thanks be to God through Jesus Christ our Lord!" (Rom. 7:25).

Use in the Reformed Tradition and the Presbyterian Church

For Presbyterians, the importance of the concept of justification by faith alone cannot be overstated. The need for its renewed understanding is a central feature of our constitution, especially in the *Book of Confessions:*

> The Presbyterian Church (U.S.A.) states its faith and bears witness to God's grace in Jesus Christ in the creeds and confessions in the *Book of Confessions.* . . . In its confessions, the Presbyterian Church (U.S.A.) identifies with the affirmations of the Protestant Reformation. The focus of these affirmations is the rediscovery of God's grace in Jesus Christ as revealed in the Scriptures. The Protestant watchwords—grace alone, faith alone, Scripture alone—embody principles of understanding which continue to guide and motivate the people of God in the life of faith. (G-2.0100; 2.0400)

Throughout its history, the Protestant church has turned to justification in its struggles against spiritual malaise and also in battles against ecclesiastical and political tyranny. As Martin Luther said in his *Preface to Romans,* the knowledge that we are saved by the love of God in Jesus Christ gives the church extraordinary courage in the most difficult circumstances. Faith, he wrote, was not something dreamed of, a human illusion, but is that which God effects in us. Faith is an unshakable confidence, a belief in the grace of God so assured that a person could die a thousand deaths for its sake. It makes us joyful, high spirited, and eager in our relations with God and all other people.[18]

In the Second Helvetic Confession (1566), believers in the midst of a violent struggle with Roman Catholics for control of Christ's church reasserted that salvation cannot be attributed to faith and actions at the same time: "We do not share in the benefit of justification partly because of the grace of God or Christ, and partly because of ourselves, our love, works or merit, but we attribute it wholly to the grace of God in Christ through faith" (C-5.110).

In the Westminster Standards justification continued to be of central importance as Presbyterians, Congregationalists, and Baptists in Scotland

and England, and commissioners from the Reformed Church in France, all tried to create a second Reformation to reform the Church of England (Westminster Confession, C-6.068–6.074; 6.019, 6.043; Shorter Catechism, 7.033; Larger Catechism, 7.180–83).

By 1934 the doctrine of justification took on critical political significance as some Christians in Germany resisted a Nazi government determined to stifle, control, and ultimately destroy the Christian church. Rejecting the idea that the church could ever have any leaders (Führer) other than Christ (C-8.21), the writers of the Theological Declaration of Barmen also turned aside the false doctrine that there are areas in life in which believers would not belong to Jesus Christ but to other lords, "areas in which we would not need justification and sanctification through him" (C-8.15).

> The Church's commission, upon which its freedom is founded, consists in delivering the message of the free grace of God to all people in Christ's stead, and therefore in the ministry of his own Word and work through sermon and Sacrament. We reject the false doctrine, as though the Church in human arrogance could place the Word and work of the Lord in the service of any arbitrarily chosen desires, purposes, and plans. (C-8.26–27)[19]

In more recent years, the church's central commitment to the concept of justification by faith has returned to some of the theological issues debated during the Reformation. Recognizing the fact that differences of opinion about the way in which Christians are saved has done more than divide Catholics and Protestants—it has also separated Protestants from each other—a formula of agreement was reached between the Evangelical Lutheran Church in America, the Presbyterian Church (U.S.A.), the Reformed Church in America, and the United Church of Christ, and was approved by subsequent General Assemblies in 1997 and 1998. In this agreement, the signers agree to a full communion that withdraws historic conditions of hostility that have divided the churches in the past. A section entitled "A Fundamental Doctrinal Consensus" declares that a basis of the proposal includes justification, the sacraments, ministry, and the church and the world. "On Justification, participants in the first dialogue agreed 'that each tradition has sought to preserve the wholeness of the Gospel as including forgiveness of sins and renewal of life' . . . ; that 'there are no substantive matters concerning justification that divide us.'"[20]

In October 1999, Lutheran and Roman Catholic leaders gathered in Augsburg, Germany, and similarly declared that justification is no longer a doctrine that divides these branches of the Christian church either. Recalling the tremendous animosity that has prevailed historically between Protestants and

Catholics concerning issues of justification and works, both churches declared that believers are saved by grace alone. Whether or not this agreement will stand remains to be seen. A document issued by the Vatican on September 5, 2000, *Declaration Dominus Jesus,* states that those who have not received salvation through the Roman Catholic Church "are gravely deficient" in comparison to those who have "the fulness of the means of salvation," and stated that "ecclesial communities which have not preserved valid episcopate and the genuine and integral substance of the eucharistic mystery are not churches in the proper sense."[21] A meeting held in Rome on February 4, 2001, among representatives of Roman Catholic, Lutheran, and Reformed churches reopened dialogue with the discussion of the issue of indulgences, in order to clarify the historical, theological, and pastoral concerns that this teaching creates, but additional agreements were not formulated at that time.[22] Further discussion in March, 2001 between a delegation from the PC(USA) and Pope John Paul II clarified mutual concerns significantly. The conversation was partially based on a paper primarily prepared by the Rev. Lew Mudge and the Rev. Anna Case-Winters that represented Presbyterian concerns ("The Successor to Peter"). As a joint statement of the Presbyterian participants and the Pontifical Council for Promoting Christian Unity later put it, it was agreed that the two churches would continue to work on the possibility of Reformed involvement in the development of an ecumenical consensus on the doctrine of justification, building on the Lutheran and Roman Catholic model. It was also hoped that it might be possible to reach a mutual recognition of baptism, and a continuing study of the events in the past that have divided Protestants and Roman Catholics. As the Stated Clerk, the Rev. Clifton Kirkpatrick, said in a presentation to the Pope, "We seek to move beyond the condemnations of our past history and to be able to affirm one another as true churches of Jesus Christ. In a fragmented world, we feel a particular urgency to witness together to the unifying love of Jesus Christ for a suffering and divided humanity."[23] Dialogue continues by other means as Presbyterians officially participate in ecumenical conversations through the World Alliance of Reformed Churches and other organizations.

Prospects: How Can the Text Be Rightly Used in the Future?

What relevance will the concept of justification by faith alone have as Presbyterians move into the future? Clearly it will have an impact on the question of ecumenism. But what about the development of spirituality and a sense of God's justice?

When Martin Luther rediscovered Paul's teaching about the free gift of forgiveness through Jesus Christ, it provided a powerful antidote to the sense of guilt that permeated much of his life and strengthened him spiritually. In his own struggle against sin and the devil, Luther sometimes believed strongly and other times suffered deepest doubts. In 1527 he wrote to Melanchthon, "For more than a week I have been thrown back and forth in death and Hell; my whole body feels beaten, my limbs are still trembling. I almost lost Christ completely, driven about on the waves and storms of despair and blasphemy against God. But because of the intercession of the faithful, God began to take mercy on me and tore my soul from the depths of Hell."[24] Although he expressed how difficult it is to understand that salvation is a mystery, that our justification is hidden in God,[25] Luther ultimately learned that the just shall *live* by faith, rather than thinking that "in the midst of life we are surrounded by death." Luther's faith enabled him "to vigorously turn this on its head: 'In the midst of death we are surrounded by life.' "[26]

For Christians of the future who will no doubt struggle with their own guilt, Luther's faith could provide a powerful example. But how will such guilt express itself? Is it possible, as John Leith suggests, that we will feel guilty about the things we are not really guilty for, and be anxious about those things that are not our fault ?[27] Or will we worry about salvation at all? While many people may think that it is unnecessary to be concerned about sin, concluding that although they may have faults and weaknesses they are really not so bad after all, Leith points out that some believers suffer from enormous guilt already because they are not good parents, they are unsuccessful in social relationships, or they have not achieved what they want in their careers. People who have a deep disparity between what life could be and what it is often end up in despair. Such uncertainty is not assuaged by the complexity of modern life and the pace at which most people are forced to live, since those who work long hours and have little time to build relationships do not have the luxury of wondering about God's love or how they can help their neighbors. Many of them have no free time to pray or think about faith at all, or so it seems, and the prospect of attending worship or participating in a Bible study is merely one more demand on a crushing schedule. Those who are judged constantly by the time they put in at work, by their productivity or billable hours, will find it hard to believe that God could accept and forgive them simply on the basis of forgiveness in Christ. Nowhere else in life, they would say, allows them the luxury of love as the final judge.

The reverse is also possible. People who work hard, obey the law, invest in the stock market, purchase the latest computer equipment at will, communicate regularly with people throughout the world via the Internet, and have the financial freedom to save securely for retirement may develop what Leith calls a "new righteousness" that looks down on others who appear lazy, have little money, and break social codes or the law. Those who are less well off, it may be judged, do not deserve God's love and favor because they have not accumulated enough points in the game of life. A world and a church that is permeated by a materialist works-righteousness may need a Reformation of its own before it can realize that it too is only saved by a loving God and not by what it produces, accomplishes, or lists on a résumé.

Concern about this problem is nothing new to Presbyterians. With pre-science, John Calvin warned believers to be ready to seize God's grace when they have cast out confidence in themselves. Empty yourselves, he said, not of righteousness, which exists not, but of "a vain and airy semblance of righteousness." To the extent that we rest satisfied with ourselves, we impede the beneficence of God.[28]

In his book *Paul the Apostle to America,* Robert Jewett suggests that the struggle between law and freedom also has other important ramifications in the life of the church in the future (i.e., through the loss of individual freedom and individuality). Paul, he argues, thought that he was saved before he met Christ, not by striving to be unique but by being a conformist. By conforming perfectly to the law, and being like all other observant Jews, Paul was convinced that he could surely please God.[29] What he needed to be relieved of, Jewett argues, was not a guilty conscience about noncompliance with the law, but from conformity itself. The chief thing that keeps Americans from a vital relationship with God is not our guilt but our absolute certainty that we are right if we are like everyone else. If we feel threatened every time we fall behind in the search for status and prestige, we act in a way that will allow us to get ahead of others and keep ahead. The only way that Christians will be able to overcome this new conformity to the law, Jewett contends, will be to realize that "newness of Spirit" is not to be understood individually or competitively, and that being free does not mean we all dress alike with our labels facing outward, but in the realization that we are all one in Christ: "When people are set free from the spirit of consumerism, they become capable for the first time of sustaining genuine relationships. The spirit of Christ constantly conveys to our fearful hearts that we are beloved whether we conform or not."[30]

A final future perspective comes from the third world. Elsa Tamez, professor of theology at the Seminario Biblico Latinamericano in Costa Rica, balances Paul's view of justification with that found in Jas. 2:14–17. Realizing that you cannot be saved if your faith never translates into action, Tamez challenges contemporary Christians from the point of view of the poor and oppressed.[31] How, she asks, can we really know God if we think of salvation only in individualistic terms? It is shameful to bring the message of saving individual souls to people who are not really the sinners of the world but its victims. How can we dare to say to the oppressed of Latin American—the poor, native people, blacks, mestizos, and women—that God loves them and justifies them when we do nothing to identify the faces of those in oppressive governments or corporations that exploit them?

Justification, Tamez argues, involves more than cheap grace for those who want to do whatever they want to do. It involves God's justice, because without it there can be no justification or affirmation. The church, she contends, must change its concept of itself and become a community that does not act because it hopes, but hopes because it acts. Become a church, she pleads, that truly follows Jesus and sees society as a place where people can be reconciled and transformed and freed, a place where we do not just concentrate on ourselves and wonder about our own salvation, but are able to be so free in Christ that both hands are in use for the other.

Clearly the concept of justification by faith alone will continue to be a central issue for the church of the future, but perhaps not for all the reasons we may have at first suspected. Certainly its continual reexamination will force us to look beyond our own abilities and plans to see what God would have us do in the world that is just coming over the horizon, especially if we realize that our justification also must actively pursue God's justice for all of our brothers and sisters throughout the world. Perhaps, as my poem about salvation suggests, our rethinking will enable us to move beyond what we are saved from to what we are saved for.

> God
> Savior
> Messiah
> Do not save me
> Like a stamp
> Or an antique
> Collectible
> Precious
> Packed away
> For no
> Future use.
>
> But save me
> From my sin
> From myself
> From my pain and torture

From my enemies
From my misunderstandings
From my good intentions.

Save me
For your kingdom
For your people
For deliverance
For life.

God
Savior
Messiah
Save me.

Questions for Study and Reflection

1. Why is it important for Christians to know that they are forgiven by God? Can you think of times in your life when it was vitally important for you to feel God's forgiving love?
2. Do you think that the concept of being justified by faith alone is as important for persons today as it was for Paul or Martin Luther?
3. Do the majority of people take sin seriously today? Which is more important—to understand sin as it applies to you personally, or as it applies in a community or national sense?

Chapter 3

In the Beginning
Genesis 1:1–2:4

*In the beginning when God created the heavens and the earth, the
earth was a formless void and darkness covered the face of the deep,
while a wind from God swept over the face of the waters. Then God
said, "Let there be light;" and there was light.*

Centrality of the Text

The accounts of creation in Gen. 1:1–2:4 and 2:4–24 have been a major
source of discussion and disagreement for Presbyterians and other Christians
for nearly four centuries as they have struggled to understand the origins of
the universe within the context of the Christian faith. Although the Westminster Confession (1648) declares that it is an article of belief that God created
the whole universe in exactly six days (C-6.022), thinking began to change
following the publication of Charles Darwin's *On the Origin of the Species*
(1859) and the development of various theories of evolution in subsequent
years, as well as the use of source criticism as a method to study the Pentateuch in the late 1800s and beyond. It became increasingly difficult for Christians to accept the Genesis narratives as pure history or a scientific description
of the precise sequence of creative events. After years of debate, the view of
most Presbyterians was expressed by the PCUS General Assembly in 1969
when literal interpretations of Gen. 1–3 previously endorsed by the church
were officially abandoned: "Our responsibility as Christians is to deal seriously with the theories and findings of all scientific endeavors, evolution
included, and to enter into open dialogue with responsible persons involved
in scientific tasks. . . ." Even though the theory of evolution was neither
affirmed nor denied, the Assembly stated, "We conclude that the true relation
between the evolutionary theory and the Bible is that of non-contradiction and

that the position stated by the General Assemblies of 1886, 1888, 1889, and 1924 was in error and no longer represents the mind of our Church."[1]

Presbyterian understanding of the first three chapters of Genesis has been of ongoing significance in subsequent years and will continue to be important throughout the rest of the twenty-first century, since our faith about the creation influences the way we interact with our planet. Statements about the nature of God as Creator, concepts of the creation of the earth, and our understanding of human responsibility to preserve nature will impact the way we treat the environment, influence how we respond to the new discoveries revealed in human genome research, give us direction as we travel in and out of our solar system, and provide guidelines as we coexist with other living creatures. Perennial debates about theories of "creationism" and the proper way to teach earth science and biology courses in schools and colleges indicate that these texts will remain of critical importance.

The Text

Genesis 1:1–2:4 is one of the most lyrical and moving passages in the Bible. "In the beginning" sets the tone for both the Hebrew Scriptures and the Christian canon by drawing believers to consider the origin of all things, organic and inorganic. It focuses attention on God's place in the universe and the interaction of the Creator in our individual and corporate lives. Whether the first verse is translated "in the beginning" or "in a beginning"[2] is probably not critical for us. As we explore the edges of our solar system, as we peer out with the Hubble telescope to view the beginnings of the big bang some twelve to fifteen billion light years in the past, as we formulate new theories about parallel and nonconvergent universes, as we try to fathom the mystery of "dark matter," we gain new perspectives on who we are and who has made us.

It is not hard to imagine why believers in the past might have wanted to understand the days of creation in Gen. 1:1–2:4 in a literal sense. Somehow God seems more powerful and trustworthy if everything is thought to have been created in a mere 144 hours and the Bible can be assumed to be scientifically accurate.

But discoveries in the last two centuries demonstrate that such a perspective is incompatible with modern scientific knowledge. Although some Christians still insist on believing that the earth was created in 4004 B.C.,[3] geological radio carbon dating and constantly changing archaeological finds in Africa and Australia push back the origins of human beings more than seven million years (*Sahelanthropus tchadensis*) and make literalistic interpretations of the Bible more than scientifically unacceptable. Indeed, the inability to acknowledge the significance of clear evidence reveals a stubborn refusal to deal with facts, and a fear that the revelation of God's truth in the Bible cannot be compatible with its discovery in any other sphere of knowledge.

A correct understanding of the nature of Gen. 1–3 demonstrates, moreover, that a literal interpretation of these verses is also incompatible with the way in which these narratives were first written and edited. Most biblical scholars agree that Gen. 1:1–2:24 is not just one story about the origin of the universe but two separate versions of creation written by two different authors (or groups of writers), using different Hebrew words to describe God. Both writers develop unique theological descriptions of the creative process.[4] The break comes after the first half of 2:4a beginning with the words "These are the generations of the heavens," where the second story of creation is introduced.[5] One account is concerned with the creation in six days out of nothing, whereas the second focuses on the more familiar narrative about the origin of the archetypal man and woman (Adam and Eve) and the manner in which sin disrupts the relationship between humans and their God.

Although the accounts are clearly dissimilar and it is necessary to understand how and why they must be distinguished from one another, recent biblical research points out that the differences between the two narratives have often been overdrawn. Since in the final canonical form of Genesis an editor has woven the two strands together in such a nearly seamless fashion that even sophisticated modern readers often fail to notice a break at Gen. 2:4b unless they are forewarned, contemporary commentators often urge readers to focus more on the factors that unite the two stories than on those that separate them.

Generally it is assumed that both texts were written in response to creation myths from Sumeria, Akkadia, Egypt, and Canaan that were developed long before Israel became a people.[6] Genesis 1–3 makes it clear, however, that unlike some of the earlier stories, these chapters express the confidence that it was no longer true to say that the universe began through the mating of divine beings or because of pernicious squabbles in a distant heavenly court. No, the universe was created through the loving, graceful, and creative act of one God who has been known throughout history to those chosen to be the people of God. To say that God stands at the beginning of all things and that this God of Abraham, Isaac, and Jacob is also the God of David, Solomon, Mary, Jesus, and Paul is to perceive a central truth. The universe, our planet, and we ourselves exist not by chance, not by a lucky clash of chemicals, not just by "buckyballs" arriving from outer space, but through the hand of one who intentionally made a universe and a space wherein we live and move and have our being.

Genesis is best understood if we appreciate the fact that the view of the cosmos shared by the authors of the first three chapters differs considerably from our own. Since the narratives represent symbolic cosmologies acceptable when the text was written (probably that of a two-dimensional, three-tier universe) and compatible with ancient views of science,[7] it is unreasonable for twenty-first-century Christians to hold the writers of Genesis accountable to contemporary standards of mathematical proof as if they were responsible for proving a theory in a modern scientific journal. The texts of Genesis do not represent the calculus of creation, but the love behind it; not the quantum physics that helps explain the big bang, but the passion that brought it into being.

Genesis 1:24–32 is a particularly pivotal passage for understanding the first creation narrative. Christians have especially pondered the meaning of verses 26–27, where it is said that human beings were made in God's image, male and female they were created as one humanity.[8] But what does it mean to be created in God's image? Does it signify that we look like God in our physical appearance? Probably not, since verse 27 tells us that the image of God does not correspond to any known human physique but to two different people together, male and female. We know from other passages, moreover, that God can be described in ways that move far beyond anatomical terms (1 John 4:8, "God is love"). Is the image of God a more abstract construct? Does it mean that we alone in the animal kingdom have the ability to plan ahead? Are we the only creatures that have the knowledge that death is inevitable? Are we the only living beings made by God who have the spiritual capacity to interact with the Creator?

Possibly many of these aspects enter into having God's image, but beyond them, as verse 31 clearly indicates, it also means that God's stamp on us is not exclusively male or uniquely female, but both together in a living fusion. There is some quality in human beings, as they enter into the mysterious bond that exists between them, that gives us a glimpse, no matter how limited or obscured, of what God is truly like (Eph. 5:31–32). In fact, God's nature is probably not understood any better anywhere else, except, of course, in the person and work of Jesus Christ. At the very least, Gen. 1:26–27 demonstrates that the eternal God chooses to encounter other beings (even if they are created in time), and that the power of life consists in a very primary way in the relationship God has with others[9] and in the close connection they can experience with their Creator.

Use in the Reformed Tradition and the Presbyterian Church

In recent years, Presbyterians (along with Christians of other denominations) have repeatedly expressed deep concern about our understanding of the creation and how we are called to respond to the command to have dominion over all other living things (Gen. 1:28–30). What does it mean to have "dominion"? Does it give us freedom to exploit the environment for profit? Does it give us the right to create situations that cause other species to become extinct? Is it ethical to use the earth in such a way that we mortgage the future of generations to come?

In 1990 the 202nd General Assembly approved a seminal study that calls Christians to take responsibility for restoring creation rather than destroying it. Declaring that the world stands before an "eco-justice crisis" that puts the future in jeopardy, the Assembly urged Presbyterians to understand that human beings are obligated to have a right relationship with the Creator and the nonhuman creation. The next ten years were declared the "turnaround decade" in which critical problems such as water pollution, global warming, ozone depletion, and issues of sustainability would be seriously addressed. As the report put it,

> Responding theologically and ethically to the endangered planet, we, the 202nd General Assembly (1990), find powerful reasons for engagement in restoring God's creation
>
> > God's works are too wonderful, too ancient, too beautiful, too good to be desecrated.
> >
> > Restoring God's creation is God's own work in our time, in which God comes both to judge and to restore.
> >
> > The Creator-Redeemer calls faithful people to become engaged with God in keeping and healing the creation, human and non-human. . . .
> >
> > In this critical time of transition to a new era, God's new doing may be discerned as a call to earth-keeping, to justice, and to community.[10]

The 1990 report was not written in isolation but was the culmination of several years of careful consideration. As early as 1951, the PCUSA Assembly called upon Presbyterians to use natural resources for the good of all human beings.[11] A statement approved in 1954 urged Christian conscience to recognize that the stewardship of earth and water must involve both a land-use program and the development of a responsible public policy to resist the exploitation of natural resources. A study of the UPCUSA General Assembly (1971) recognized the presence of an ecological crisis that demanded a new "eco-ethic" which would value people and other living things over the rights of property; it called for a humanizing use of technology. Urging Presbyterians to adopt a simpler, more ethical lifestyle, the Assembly confessed that human beings have sinned against God's creation. It committed itself to seek God's shalom and wholeness, "which requires an equitable, hospitable environment for all life and envisions a revitalized human community."

In the first environmental statement of the reunited church, the 196th General Assembly (1984) declared that "human stewardship is not a dominion of mastery. It is a dominion of unequivocal love for this world. It is to be exercised with respect for the integrity of natural systems and for the limits that nature places on economic growth and material consumption."

Powerful statements and studies were approved in subsequent years by later assemblies.

1987 The United States is urged to search for acceptable, permanent high-level waste disposal sites, and churches are encouraged to seek efforts to improve the health and safety of farmers and farm workers. Churches and governing bodies within the denomination were asked to support increased research and development for alternative means of pest control other than toxic pesticides.

1989 The Presbyterian Eco-Justice Task Force published a study, based largely on the work of William Gibson of the Eco-Justice Project at Cornell University (*Keeping and Healing the Creation*), that provided biblical and theological rationale for developing programs to sustain renewable resources (croplands, grazing lands, forests, fisheries) and preserve those which were not (fuels, minerals).[12] Turning to the creation accounts in Genesis, the study asserts that "The biblical story roots the goodness of creation [Gen. 1:18, 21, 25, 31], not in its utility to the human creature, but in the fundamental claim of faith that the earth is God's creation—that the world exists by virtue of the purpose and power of the loving Redeemer who is also the Creator."

Other biblical texts are cited in support of the concept of God's delight in the creation (Pss. 104:24, 31; 50:12; 145:9, 16; 148:3, 9–13; Deut. 8:7–10) and particular attention is drawn to the connection between God's creative intentions and the redemption of humanity. The God who delivers the people of Israel during the Exodus is the same One who redeems the world from sin through Jesus Christ. Although all creation now groans (Rom. 8:22–23) under the weight of human sin and under the oppressiveness of pollution and the harm done to other living beings, God's creative process goes on, and God's love continues to do new things (Isa. 43:19). Trusting in God's care for the world and the universe, believers long for the new heaven and new earth when all things will be brought back together (Rev. 21:1–7). As the *Confession of*

1967 puts it, "God's redeeming work in Jesus Christ embraces the whole of man's [*sic*] life: social and cultural, economic and political, scientific and technological, individual and corporate. It includes man's natural environment as exploited and despoiled by sin. It is the will of God that his purpose for human life shall be fulfilled under the rule of Christ and all evil be banished from his creation" (C-9.53). *Keeping and Healing the Creation* provided the immediate impetus for the approval of *Restoring Creation for Ecology and Justice* by the next General Assembly (1990).

1996 The 208th General Assembly approved *Hope for a Global Future: Toward Just and Sustainable Human Development*, a study which presented a theological understanding of the complexities of economic justice, concerns about population, the injustice of poverty, and ecological degradation.[13] It called for human justice on a planet where many suffer scarcity in a world filled with abundance, and also demanded "biotic justice" for nonhuman creatures that share their homes with us. "This concern for justice to nonhuman life introduces a major moral limit to economic activity. Production and consumption must be limited to the carrying capacity of nature. This limitation assumes that all species are entitled to a 'fair share' of the goods necessary for their welfare and perpetuation. We need moral limits to economic activity to prevent excessive harm to wildlife and wildlands. Profligate production and consumption are abuses of what God has designed for fair and frugal use in a universal covenant of justice."[14]

1998 The 210th Assembly urged the United States to ratify the Kyoto protocol seeking to have the U.S., and all other industrial countries, reduce greenhouse emissions, and develop policies on renewable energy, fuel and energy efficiency, and reforestation.

1999 The next General Assembly reaffirmed ratification of the Kyoto treaty stating that scientific studies have clearly demonstrated the "mounting gravity of the effects upon earth and people from climate change resulting from human-induced global warming." Presbyterians were warned about the danger from increasing population, affluent lifestyles, and unsustainable economic development that could undermine the integrity of God's creation. They were encouraged to revitalize democratic institutions "for protecting against excessive concentrations of power and equitably redistributing access to the sustenance of earth intended by the Creator for all."[15]

Prospects: How Can the Text Be Rightly Used in the Future?

Although Presbyterians have found many theological, sociological, and political issues to be of extreme importance over the past few years, none are more crucial for the future than those concerned with creation. Most critical are issues that concern environmental protection and the possible dangers presented by global warming. Scientists are nearly unanimous in concluding that the continuing destruction of the ozone layer through the dumping of waste products into the atmosphere could lead to catastrophic results. In fact, some researchers think we may have gone too far and that the destruction may already be past the point of no return. Recent weather patterns show the deleterious effects of massive changes. Ecosystems are being damaged around the world as fauna and flora continue to die off at alarming rates. The specter of melting polar ice and diminishing glaciers and ice shelves haunts unborn generations.[16]

In the years ahead, every General Assembly will be negligent as a steward of God's creation if its members do not address environmental concerns in significant ways. As Bill McKibben so eloquently puts it, the church of the future must address issues surrounding the protection of our planet with as much seriousness as past generations did when they battled issues of slavery, fought against Hitler and world fascism during World War II, and worked to advance civil rights in the 1960s: "I suggest that in our time the morally transcendent question is whether we will stop this decreation before it goes further; whether we will take the steps—and some of them will be difficult steps—to preserve God's creation in as intact and integral form as is still possible. Or whether we will watch it as it unravels—which is what we are doing so far."[17] In his opinion, the timing is critical since we may have less than twenty years left to prevent disaster:

> Our story begins with the account of creation. Since we happen to be alive in the two-or-three-decade period of decreation, we have to do all that we can, whatever the cost, to defend God's work. Forget about teaching creation in the schools; in our time the task is to preserve creation on the planet. Creation is not an artifact of history. It is all around us, and it is being destroyed. Saving it is our task.[18]

As Presbyterians reflect on the creation of the universe and our place in it as human beings, we will also need to be deeply concerned about continuing DNA research, especially in regard to the new genetics and various aspects of genome research.[19] Genetics and neuroscience offer us new ways to understand ourselves and other creatures. Possibilities of altering the genetic code are announced with increasing frequency nearly every week. What kind of discoveries will be made to help prevent inherited diseases? Can infants receive significant treatment while they are still in the womb? Is it possible, on the other hand, that alterations of DNA sequences could be used in nonpeaceful ways, as weapons of biological warfare? Do we have the capacity to produce monsters as we tinker with reproductive strands? What implications arise when new methods of human fertilization make it possible for parents to choose a child's genetic makeup? As we learn more about our own stored genetic code, will we find what has sometimes been called "a mitochondrial Eve," a common DNA source that emerged from Africa hundreds of thousands of years ago? Should the stem cells of fetuses be used for research and medical treatment? Important ethical, theological, and spiritual questions will need to be raised regularly as research continues if we are to understand the relationship between discoveries in biology and evolution and our claim to be made in God's image.

As we look more deeply inward to understand our own inherited structure, Christians will also be called on in the future to look beyond the human situation to the plight of other animals that come under our dominion. Since human beings have the power to move all over the planet earth, we are indeed the only creatures able to do good or ill everywhere.[20] If human beings have the power to name other animals (Gen. 2:19–20) and exercise dominion over every living thing that moves upon the earth (Gen. 1:28–29), we also have the ability to make other creatures suffer or even cause them to become extinct. The first creation story tells us that other living creatures are truly good in God's eyes, and as we discover more and more about the intelligence of primates, dolphins, whales, and other animals, we will need to be more vocal in our opposition to what Richard Leakey calls the "current spasm of extinction."[21] Many avenues of protection must be explored, from a global fund for wildlife to increased restriction on industrial development and human settlement in areas where other creatures have their well-being and lives threatened.

As Presbyterians and other people of faith consider the future, it is likely that before long we will eventually need to broaden our horizons beyond concern for life-forms on earth to those that may exist in other solar systems or galaxies. In the first Genesis creation story, the appearance of a man and woman on the sixth and final day of creation appears to indicate that human beings stand at the apex of God's creative process. For the present, this anthropomorphic bias of the texts still makes profound sense, since we have not yet discovered life elsewhere in the universe. (Or should we say it has not chosen to reveal itself, or has not been allowed to make itself known?) But even as we consider the unique place God has given us in creation, our exploration of other areas of the Milky Way galaxy by Pioneer spacecraft, as well as our probing of distant planets with radio messages announcing our presence on earth, may change our perspective someday if we encounter other forms of intelligent life. For now, we wonder about our place in the chain of creation and are thankful for the honor God gives us, but the immensity of space and the continuing discovery of planets like earth in other galaxies should cause us to glance over our cosmic shoulder as we imagine who might sneak up behind us from an unknown corner of the universe. Changes in our perception may cause us to wonder how other beings might relate to the God who made us all.

In the future, Presbyterians must do more than merely respond to scientific discoveries and attempt to interpret them from a faith perspective. Christians must also continue to look for new ways to understand biblical creation texts and Scripture passages closely related to them. We know that many believers (most of them outside of the Reformed tradition) are very skeptical of all theories of evolution and cling tenaciously to what they consider to be the true biblical interpretations of nature. Presbyterians must continue to resist the introduction of literalist interpretations of Genesis (often called "creationism") into high school and college curricula and help children and youth understand the correct meaning of the biblical creation stories.[22] It is time, as Daniel Migliori points out, to "put the old warfare between Christian faith and science behind us."[23] Perhaps this can be done by helping modern Christians understand more clearly the many different models of creation used by believers in the past to describe the creative process.[24] It is encouraging that the 214th General Assembly asked the Office of Theology, Worship, and Discipleship to develop new resources on the intersection of science and theology and the affirmation of God as Creator.

No doubt it will also be necessary for future generations to discover new metaphors to describe God's relationship to the creation in order to preserve the ability of Christians to "call the church to that unity in confession and mission which is required of disciples" in their own day (Confession of 1967, C-9.05).[25] New days demand new expressions of who God is and how Christ redeems the beings he seeks to save. No doubt it will be necessary to reexplore the involvement of the cosmic Christ in the beginning of all things (John 1:1–14; Col. 1:18–20), the Christian concept of the continuing process of creation, and the understanding of the connection between the resurrection and the new heaven and earth (Rom. 4:17; Rev. 21:1–7)[26] to be sure that the Reformed perspective remains thoroughly Trinitarian and Christ centered.

Above all, Presbyterians must continue to insist on the contact between ecology and justice and the necessity not only of preserving the creation but of protecting the people who are impacted by critical decisions yet to be made. Choices about conservation, industrial development, and future methods of producing energy must be made without ruining the lives of the human beings who will be effected by them in the next centuries. As Holmes Rolson III puts it,

> The Bible is a book about how to live justly, not about how natural history works. The righteous life depicted there is not simply how to go to heaven, prominent as the kingdom of heaven is in the New Testament; the righteous life, especially in the Old Testament, is about a long life on earth, sustainable until the third and fourth generations. . . . The Bible is about a gap between what *is* and what *ought to be,* and how to close that gap.[27]

Questions for Study and Reflection

1. Are you aware of any controversies in your community about the concepts of evolution or creationism? Have they been resolved?
2. Have you seen any evidence of global warming or environmental pollution in your area? Is your church or presbytery involved in eco-justice projects to rectify these problems?
3. What does your congregation do to support environmental protection? Do you use eco-friendly lighting and heating?
4. Do you agree that questions about eco-justice are the most pressing theological issues that the contemporary church faces? If not, how do you evaluate the clear and pressing danger of global warming and environmental pollution?

Chapter 4

Those Predestined Were Also Called
Romans 8:30

And those whom he predestined he also called; and those whom he called he also justified; and those whom he justified he also glorified.

Centrality of the Text

*I*t is ironic that a doctrine most often associated with Presbyterians is one specifically rejected by the UPCUSA in 1903. Even in the 1940s, church historians could safely state that it was common for people outside of the denomination to say, "Presbyterians believe in predestination!"[1] And at the beginning of the twenty-first century it is still not unusual for believers from other churches to ask, "Is your church the one that believes that God decides who is saved and who is not?"

What non-Presbyterians are referring to, of course, is not the biblical concept of election found in Romans and Ephesians (see the discussion below) but the Reformed concept of double predestination. In order to make this distinction clearer, the order of the discussion of the biblical texts and the development of Reformed and Presbyterian doctrine will be reversed in this chapter.

Use in the Reformed Tradition and the Presbyterian Church

First formulated by Augustine, "double predestination" was adopted by Protestant leaders to distinguish their theology from the Roman Catholic concept of salvation through works. It had a particular appeal to the legal mind of John Calvin. To him it was only logical: If God calls some people to salvation and we are only saved by the free gift of love in Christ, it must also follow that God is the one who chooses to damn others to the torments of hell. Although Calvin firmly believed in the concept of human free will and demanded that people accept responsibility for their sin, he also knew that God was sovereign in the world and that nothing happened without divine intervention. For him it was unthinkable that the positive parts of life could be attributed to God but that negative aspects were outside heavenly control. As he puts it in a passage often quoted from *Institutes of the Christian Religion* (3.21.5),

> We call predestination God's eternal decree, by which he determined within himself what he willed to become of each man. For all are not created in equal condition; rather, eternal life is foreordained for some, eternal damnation for others. Therefore, as any man has been created to one or the other of these ends, we speak of him as predestined to life or to death.[2]

Although Calvin's cold, analytical position may seem hard-hearted, it must be remembered that here interest is not focused so much on the nature of God as it is on the centrality of the doctrine of justification by faith alone (see chapter 2). Calvin and the other reformers wanted to demonstrate by all means that God was the only one who could offer salvation. There was no other way to be saved (especially by works of righteousness) except through the free gift in Christ. The very fact that it might seem to be unfair demonstrated more clearly that it was free (3.21.6).

Certainly not all Christians accepted Calvin's argument. The doctrine of double predestination is not found in the earliest creeds; it does not appear in chapter 8 of the Scots Confession (1560), in the Heidelberg Catechism (1563), or in the Second Helvetic Confession (1566).[3] Although his position was meant to emphasize the goodness of God rather than provide a way to divide one section of society from another, Calvinists who used his writings in later years to develop an "absolutist and rationalist system-building spirit"[4] pushed his concept to extremes. Christians who found the idea of God condemning people to damnation repulsive and un-Christian (especially the Arminians) were strongly refuted by statements incorporated in the Westminster Standards (1647). In the third chapter of the Westminster Confession, for example, it is asserted that

> God from all eternity did by the most wise and holy counsel of his own free will, freely and unchangeably ordain whatsoever comes to pass; yet so as thereby neither is God the author of sin; nor is violence offered to the will of the creatures. . . . By the decree of God, for the manifestation of his glory, some men and angels are predestinated unto eternal life, and others are fore-

ordained to everlasting death. These angels and men, thus predestinated and fore-ordained, are particularly and unchangeably designed; and their number is so certain and definite that it cannot be either increased or diminished. (C-6.014; C-6.016-6.017)

It is not surprising that this kind of severe salvation calculus was rejected by many believers, Presbyterians included. Obviously it undermined the possibility of repentance and made the growing interest in worldwide missions appear to be fruitless.[5] The effort to convert non-Christians to the gospel might even be seen as contrary to God's will if those in other countries were already counted among the damned. Resistance to the concept became particularly strong during the latter part of the nineteenth century when Presbyterians made several attempts to revise the Westminster Standards. The issue was heated, and once again there were those who feared that the church would split.[6] The debate was even more severe than it might have been since it was connected with heresy charges brought against prominent seminary professors.[7] Although enough presbyteries did not approve suggested amendments in 1893, by 1903 the climate had changed (and some compromises were reached), and the addition of chapter 34, "Of the Holy Spirit"; chapter 35, "On the Gospel of the Love of God and Missions"; and a "Declaratory Statement" effectively removed double predestination from Presbyterian faith and practice. Supported by leading Presbyterian theologians, an associate justice of the Supreme Court, and a former president of the United States (Benjamin Harrison[8]), the Declaratory Statement made the new position strikingly clear: "With reference to Chapter III of the Confession of Faith: that concerning those who are saved in Christ, the doctrine of God's eternal decree is held in harmony with the doctrine of his love to all mankind, his gift of his Son to be the propitiation for the sins of the whole world, and his readiness to bestow his saving grace on all who seek it . . ." (C-6.192). Asserting that God never prevents people from accepting the gospel, the amendment concludes by flatly rejecting the idea that children who die as babies are sent to hell: "We believe that all dying in infancy are included in the election of grace, and are regenerated and saved by Christ through the Spirit, who works when and where and how he pleases" (C-6.193).

The Text

The major New Testament texts that deal with the concept of predestination are Rom. 8:29–30 and Eph. 1:5, 11, verses where the Greek verb *proorizō* is used to describe God's decisions about events before they happen.[9] The texts in Romans are mainly concerned with the doctrine of election, that is, the call of God that is extended to those whom God chooses. Those whom God foreknew have been conformed to the image of the Son. The ones who are predestined are called, those called are justified, and those justified are also glorified.

Here Paul's understanding, unlike the doctrine of double predestination, does not have two cutting edges, since his motive is primarily positive. His purpose is made clear in 8:28: "We know that all things work together for good for those who love God, who are called" according to God's purpose.

The section comprised of chapters 8–11, in fact, in spite of its complexity, deals mainly with the question of who is saved rather than who is not. These chapters provide pillars of hope because they demonstrate how great God's love really is. Those who have been called to believe understand what is meant intuitively. Despite the fact that Christians have to respond to the gospel in order to become followers of Christ (what Mark 1:15 calls repentance), they know that there is something mysterious and inevitable about their decision, that they are not so much making a choice as they are being chosen (John 15:16).

How this happens precisely is difficult to explain. Believers have to make choices, but so does God. Just as the prophets were called by God to their special work (Jer. 1:5; Isa. 6; 49:1; 1 Sam. 1:22, 28) and could not do it unless God did the calling, they still had to respond. In the New Testament, Jesus selects his disciples and even gives them new names on occasion (see Mark 3:13–15). Yet they still have to decide to leave fishing and tax collecting to do his bidding. Later followers of Jesus had the same ineffable feeling: In regard to their own decisions about ministry, God was the one who took the initiative (Rom. 1:1; 1 Cor. 1:1; Gal. 1:1, 15), and they were the ones who answered.[10]

In Rom. 9–11 Paul struggles with the ramifications of this difficult balance between God's choice and our choices. There he is forced to wonder out loud about who is saved and who is not. He is compelled to deal with it because it appears that his people, the Jewish people, the people of the covenant, are *not* saved, since the majority of them have not accepted Jesus Christ as Lord and Savior.

Here he is not contemplating some ice-cold mathematical formula that determines who is in and who is out. For Paul it is intensely existential. The people he is talking about are his people. They comprise his family, his roots, his heritage. They are neighbors and friends. In 9:2–3 he expresses his agony in the most painful personal terms and wishes that he could bear the judgment coming their way: "I have great sorrow and unceasing anguish in my heart.

For I could wish that I myself were accursed and cut off from Christ for the sake of my own people, my kindred according to the flesh."

In the rest of the verses in Rom. 9–11, he tries to formulate a satisfactory solution as he records the debate taking place in his own heart. What is to become of his own people? How could God reject those who were called from the beginning? How could a loving God do such a thing? Yet how can it happen otherwise if they do not believe in Jesus (10:14, 21)? In 10:1 he makes his own desire clear—"my heart's desire and prayer to God for them is that they may be saved"—and in 11:1–6 expresses his final conclusion worked out in an agonizing fashion. "By no means" has God cast aside the people of Israel, the ones given the first covenant. God has not rejected his people whom God foreknew" (11:2). A remnant has been saved, chosen by God's grace (11:5–7).

Just how Paul finally works out the dilemma in detail is not clear and is often debated by commentators. Some Bible scholars think that he accepts a kind of universalism: God has imprisoned all people in disobedience so that mercy may be extended to all (11:32). Others suggest that he sees Israel's salvation taking place primarily through Christ's ingrafting of the non-Jewish branch of the human family into God's covenant plant (the main root, 11:17–25) and, by making the Jews jealous, driving them to Jesus (11:14–15), ultimately including all of God's children in the covenant. A third position argues that the remnant saved only includes those Jews who finally accept Christ and enter the kingdom through the new covenant of grace.

Whatever Paul finally decides, it is clear that his great hope is quite different and much more humane than the cold rationality of the concept of double predestination, that God calculates who will be saved and who will be damned before they are even born. For Paul, love will ultimately win out and even death will not be able to separate the children from God in Jesus Christ (8:37–39). Finally, somehow in some way, all will be embraced in the love of God. It is possible that Paul does not know exactly how this happens. For him the fact that some of his own people have hardened their hearts is a "mystery" (11:25). But even their disobedience will lead to acceptance, through the gospel. It is amazing, but all things fit together in God's plan for all people, Gentiles and Jews together, even if an initial response is negative: "Just as you were once disobedient to God but have now received mercy because of their disobedience, so they have now been disobedient in order that, by the mercy shown to you, they too may receive mercy. For God has imprisoned all in disobedience "in order to extend mercy to all" (11:30–32).

Finally, in Rom. 11:33–36, Paul can do nothing more than leave the matter in the hands of a God who can be trusted to work all things out. At the end, rational analysis is suspended and he concludes his discussion with a beautiful doxology that merely heaps praise on the Lord. "O the depth of the riches and wisdom and knowledge of God!" (v. 33). To God " be the glory forever. Amen" (v. 36).

In the second major biblical passage involving predestination, a similar conclusion that centers on the ultimate goodness of God is found in the later discussion of one of Paul's disciples in Ephesians. As Ernest Best points out in his impressive commentary, the purpose of that book is also positive, since the emphasis in Eph. 1:3–6 is on love rather than judgment: "Blessed be the God and Father of our Lord Jesus Christ, who has blessed us in Christ with every spiritual blessing in the heavenly places, just as [God] chose us in Christ before the foundation of the world to be holy and blameless before [God]in love." As Best puts it, "The reference to love implies that God's purpose originates in and is controlled by . . . love; it is not an arbitrary exercise of power. . . . God's foreordination began in . . . love: it results in the praise of . . . grace."[11] In Eph. 1:3–14, believers have been adopted as God's children according to divine "good pleasure" and, like Paul, the author of Ephesians can only end his comments on being chosen from the beginning with words of praise: Having been destined according to God's purpose, we have obtained an inheritance according to God's counsel and will "so that we, who were the first to set our hope on Christ, might live for the praise" of God's glory (1:12).

Prospects: How Can the Text Be Rightly Used in the Future?

A proper understanding of the biblical texts in Romans and Ephesians helps us formulate our own beliefs today. As Presbyterians, we know that God calls us to service. We also know that evil exists in the world, and because God's will is not always accomplished, we have to pray for it every single day. We realize that non-Christians must hear the good news in order to come to Christ (Rom. 10), but we also know that some do not respond in a positive way (see Mark 4:13–20). How some come to God and others do not may finally remain mysterious. How God regards those who believe in other religions may not be something we fully understand. All we can do is give thanks that we are aware of God's love in Christ, that we know on whom our own salvation rests, and hope and trust in God to take care of all of the other children who are far away. Perhaps it is fair to say that it is not our responsibility to spend our time trying to figure out whom God loves or rejects. If we consider all human beings to be children of God, and treat them that way, we can remove the anxiety of this kind of speculative judgment and leave all final determination to the one who created us all.

Beyond the interest in questions of salvation, of course, the main premise behind the concept of predestination, that is, belief in the overarching power of God, still elicits great interest in contemporary culture even if it is not always expressed in biblical terms. In addition to the tremendous fascination still exhibited by believers in predestination (there are thousands of entries extant on the Internet, as the simple use of any search engine reveals), it is not unusual, when there is a death in a family or a tragedy, for people to ask one another, even if they have no connection with Christianity or any other religion, "Why did God do this to me? What did I do to deserve this? Why do bad things happen to good people?"

From other perspectives, the concept of having life controlled by outside forces is expressed in terms that are not spiritually oriented at all. In movies it is still popular to create scripts that indicate that "the force" is with us, that angels or the spirits of departed loved ones are influencing us, that some power from a distant galaxy is manipulating us, or that a meteor speeding toward earth will seal our future. In some ways, modern men and women believe more in the ancient concept of fate dramatized by Sophocles in *Oedipus Rex* or have more faith in superstition or astrology than they do in the power of the living God. Often we wonder if there are forces in life so strong that they can make people do the very thing they do not want to do. What is more, modern culture often speculates about interior impulses that act as determinants. Are we in control of our own futures, or are we on prescribed courses set by individual personality types—merely the function of our Myers-Briggs profiles or our DNA makeup?

Presbyterians believe that the power that influences our destiny comes from the God who has ultimate charge of the universe, and that God, not some impersonal force, is "the free determiner of all that comes to pass in the world."[12] We believe that God's sovereign love is beyond our understanding and that God chose to transform the world through the Redeemer who made all things to serve the purpose of this love (Confession of 1967, C-9.15). We confess that we trust in God and state,

> In everlasting love, the God of Abraham and Sarah chose a covenant people to bless all families of the earth. Hearing their cry, God delivered the children of Israel from the house of bondage. Loving us still, God makes us heirs with Christ of the covenant. Like a mother who will not forget her nursing child, like a father who runs to welcome the prodigal home, God is faithful still. (Brief Statement of Faith, C-10.3)

In our own lifetimes, some of us have seen how faith in God's foreknowledge and power is played out. When I was the pastor of First Presbyterian

Church in Plattsburgh, New York, some of our members were connected with the large Strategic Air Command base in that community. Many Air Force personnel were convinced that the Soviet Union was a monolithic, evil power that would always threaten the free world. To them it was inconceivable that the Soviet peril would ever disappear or that SAC would be out of business. Yet many Christians struggled and prayed for unilateral disarmament and for world peace even at the bleakest moments. Looking back, it is possible now to see God's power at work, a force that reduced nuclear arms, helped bring down the Berlin Wall, and may have sparked the disintegration of the Soviet Union. The forces of popular opinion, military might, and industrial profit-sharing were so much against these possibilities, how else are such developments finally to be explained? As a result of these developments, SAC was no longer necessary and the hand on the nuclear clock was pushed backward a few minutes.

In the private lives of believers, it is also possible with hindsight to see God's providence at work. Even though we wonder at times why God puts us in certain places at specific times, or why pastors or elders are called to serve particular congregations, we often can look back and see a pattern, a plan, a process, that can only be attributed to God's desire to work out all things for good.

Presbyterians also know, of course, that although God does work in the world, God's will is not always inevitable in the immediate sense, even if it is inevitable in the final sense.[13] God's will can be thwarted by sin, apathy, laziness, illness, natural disasters, war, and evil intent. Human beings have the freedom to ignore God and even work against divine purposes. Yet it is possible to believe and know that ultimately God's will is going to be fulfilled in Jesus Christ, even if it has to pass through the agony of the cross to be realized. We may not attribute the result to predestination, or understand exactly how that will happen, but we know that it certainly has to do with the final plan of God to work all things together for good.

Questions for Study and Reflection
   1. Read through Rom. 9–11 and the first chapter of Ephesians. Does the main point in these chapters concern God's foreknowledge of our salvation, or the love in Christ that makes it possible?
   2. Do you believe that God has your life all laid out for you in detail right up to the point of death? Or do you think that free will and prayer can change things? If God does guide our lives as Christians, how do you reconcile the two possibilities?
   3. Do you believe that it is God's will that some people will die in tragic accidents or because of fatal illnesses? If God wills these kinds of things, where is love? If God does not guide our lives, where is God's power?

Chapter 5

Let My People Go
Exodus 5:1

Moses and Aaron went to Pharaoh and said, "Thus says the LORD, the God of Israel, 'Let my people go, so that they may celebrate a festival to me in the wilderness.'"

Centrality of the Text

When Israel was in Egypt's land,
Let my people go!
Oppressed so hard they could not stand,
Let my people go!
Go down, Moses,
Way down in Egypt's land,
Tell old Pharaoh,
Let my people go![1]

*T*he words of this African American spiritual summarize the pleas, prayers, and hymns for freedom of many people around the world who have expressed over the centuries the universal human yearning for liberty under God.

The text is derived from the story of Israel's liberation from Egyptian bondage when Moses proclaims God's command to case-hardened Pharaoh. Repeated several times to an oppressor refusing to surrender power (Exod. 6:10; 7:16; 8:1–2; 9:1, 13), the warning is not heeded until God strikes where it hurts the most, and the firstborn are lost. Lest dictators and tinhorns of any age fail to understand that God's words apply more than just to Pharaoh, are a demand and not a request, an imperative and not a plea, and are universal and not particular, recent translations have a fresh, contemporary ring: "YHWH said to Moshe: Come to Pharaoh and speak to him 'Thus says YHWH, the God of the Hebrews: 'Send free my people, that they may serve me!'" (Exod. 9:1).[2]

God's call for mercy and freedom has been echoed and reaffirmed in Presbyterian preaching, polity, and actions over the years, and nowhere more clearly than in the words of our most recent confession:

> In a broken and fearful world
> the Spirit gives us courage
> to pray without ceasing,
> to witness among all peoples to Christ as Lord and Savior,
> to unmask idolatry in Church and culture,
> to hear the voices of peoples long silenced,
> and to work with others for justice, freedom, and peace.
> (A Brief Statement of Faith, C-10.4)

Even our worship calls out to God for justice for those who cannot speak for themselves (W-7.4002), as it supports "people who seek the dignity, freedom, and respect that they have been denied."[3]

The Text

Recent interpretations of the book of Exodus and its background make it possible to understand its significance for the church in fresh ways. Just a few years ago, it was common to assume that the message of Exodus could best be explained in light of some variation of a theory developed in the nineteenth century that argued that the text is composed of material written by four different individuals (or four different groups)—J (Yahwist), E (Elohist), D (Deuteronomist), and P (Priestly Writer)—and assembled by a final editor.[4] In current biblical study, scholars are more uncertain about the origins of the Bible's second book. The documentary hypothesis, as the earlier theory is called, is being found to be less and less useful, and commentators now turn to literary criticism, social criticism, and canonical criticism to provide better interpretations of the text and background of Exodus.[5]

Most commentators now agree that regardless of the overall interpretation given to the way Exodus was composed, its major theme is clearly liberation. Exodus tells a story, as Walter Brueggemann puts it, of the "transformation of social situations from oppression to freedom."[6] It speaks of God's presence in a way that demonstrates how social structures are changed so that the God of Israel can continue to be found in the midst of all the children of God.[7] In the giving of the Ten Commandments on Mount Sinai, God "grounds human dignity and mobilizes the strong for the weak."[8] The story of the Exodus becomes a social possibility and a social mandate for all those who read it and follow the God of Moses, as God's "awesome magisterial, life-giving glory" is seen concretely in the world.

If, as it is often argued, the book of Exodus was not written soon after Israel's deliverance from Egyptian slavery but much later during the period of Babylonian and Persian exile, it is easy to see how the continual reinterpretations of the theme "Let my people go" at various times are all legitimate—in the period prior to the American Civil War, in the struggles in South Africa, in the battle for civil rights and integration in the United States, and in the quest for freedom in Central and South America. Originally the book of Exodus itself was a reinterpretation of a powerful story that demonstrates how God appears in the history of men and women of faith to deliver them from oppression in their own time, whether the Pharaoh might be a Babylonian or Persian king, a Roman emperor,[9] slave masters in the American South, those who want to preserve the degrading practice of apartheid, promoters of racial segregation, or twenty-first century dictators. As respective Christians understand Exodus afresh for their own age, they rediscover the fact that God upholds the weak and oppressed children of God and so all theology becomes liberation theology.

Use in the Reformed Tradition and the Presbyterian Church

How was this theology of liberation expressed and worked out in practice? In three sections we will explore Christian responses to slavery in the United States, the institution of apartheid in South Africa, and the struggle for American civil rights in the twentieth century. In each case, the writings and voices of those actually involved in the debates will be heard to make it possible for us as twenty-first century Christians to consider for ourselves the passion, conviction, power, and honesty of the arguments our forebears felt compelled to make and the way they used the Scriptures to put forth their points of view.

The Question of Slavery

Although most Presbyterians realize that the church (along with the rest of the nation) split in 1861 over the issue of slavery, it is not as well known that more than seventy-four years earlier the church as a whole took a strong stand against the "peculiar" institution. On Saturday, May 26, 1787, the Synod of New York and Philadelphia received a statement from the committee of overtures recommending that they "do every thing in their power consistent with the rights of civil society, to promote the abolition of slavery, and the instruction of negroes, whether bond or free." Further,

The Creator of the world having made of one flesh all children of men, it becomes them as members of the same family, to consult and promote each other's happiness. It is more especially the duty of those who maintain the rights of humanity, and who acknowledge and teach the obligations of Christianity, to use such means as are in their power to extend the blessings of equal freedom to every part of the human race.[10]

Since it was already late in the afternoon, the matter was postponed until the next Monday morning. On May 28, presumably after considerable prayer and discussion, the Synod came to the conclusion that although approval was to be given to "the general principles in favor of universal liberty," people taken from a servile state to a position of freedom would not be ready to assume the privileges of civil society without receiving "a proper education." Therefore, it was earnestly recommended to all members of the Presbyterian church "to give those persons who are at present held in servitude," such good education as to prepare them for the better enjoyment of freedom. They further recommended that masters, wherever they find servants disposed to make a just improvement of the privilege, should either give them a *peculium,*[11] or grant them sufficient time and sufficient means to buy back their liberty at a moderate rate, in order "to procure eventually the final abolition of slavery in America."[12]

By 1815 the General Assembly was ready to make even stronger statements, condemning slave traffic as being "inconsistent with the spirit of the Gospel" and calling upon all presbyteries and sessions to make use "of all prudent measures to prevent such shameful and unrighteous conduct."[13] The 1818 General Assembly declared that slavery was a "gross violation of the most precious and sacred rights of human nature . . . utterly inconsistent with the law of God, totally irreconcilable with the spirit and principles of Christ." All Christians, it was said, must "use their honest, earnest, and unwearied endeavors to obtain the complete abolition of slavery." Any member of the Presbyterian Church who sold another human being without his or her consent was to be suspended from the church.[14]

As tensions rose in the nation, subsequent General Assemblies had little or nothing to say about slavery, hoping to avoid divisive controversy, even though the question was a principal one in the church's thoughts and prayers. As Lefferts Loetscher puts it, denominational emphases ran parallel to the political shift in the country as it moved from nationalism to sectionalism: "Starting about 1830, American life entered a new phase. The spirit of nationalism, awakened by the Revolution and fostered by the War of 1812, began to give way to a spirit of sectionalism, as the agricultural and slaveholding South and the industrial and 'free' North became more and more sharply arrayed against each other."[15]

In 1835, however, when the General Assembly met in Pittsburgh, Theodore Dwight Weld, a convert of the Finney revival and field agent of the American Anti-Slavery Society, lobbied the Assembly to support the abolitionist cause. In typical Presbyterian fashion, a committee was appointed to make an inquiry into slaveholding in the Presbyterian Church and to report back the next year.[16] By 1836 strong opposition had arisen in the South, where it was argued that the church had no business interfering in the governing of the states or in the lives of individual members. In that year the General Assembly indefinitely postponed discussion of slavery to head off the threatened departure of southern presbyteries. At the meeting in 1837, however, the General Assembly was dominated by the more conservative Old School, and the Synods of Western Reserve, Utica, Geneva, and Genesee were "exscinded" from the church. The Presbyterian Church was divided into two factions, Old School and New School.[17] Although it was stated that doctrinal errors were the primary cause of the split, every one of the excluded synods had defined slaveholding as a sin, and the questions of abolition and/or the extension of slavery into new territories had obviously become a critical issue to be faced by the church. In 1838, when the General Assembly refused to recognize the delegates from the excluded synods, they organized their own assembly while standing in the aisles and adjourned to a nearby church. Thus, two General Assemblies ended up meeting that year in Philadelphia. According to James Hastings Nichols, "Each Assembly set up some skeleton judicatories in territory dominated by the other, and each proceeded to elect Directors of Boards and in general to carry on the whole business of the church. In such fashion was celebrated the fiftieth anniversary of the founding of the General Assembly!"[18]

The desire to discontinue the discussion of the divisive issue of slavery had obviously been a failure. In 1836 the session in my own home congregation (First Presbyterian Church in Williamson, New York) took up the challenge posed by the General Assembly in 1818. After six paragraphs of preamble on the sinfulness of slavery, it was decided

> that we will not admit to our pulpit or to membership, or invite to our communion table any individual, who is a slaveholder or who traffics in human beings. Resolved that light and truth presented to the human mind, and prayer to God are our only weapons against this sin: and that we will faithfully employ them, as God shall enable us, till slavery shall cease to exist in the church, in our country and the world.[19]

Debate did not cease in the church as a whole either, and in subsequent General Assemblies the New School tried to keep northern and southern churches in one denomination. By 1857, however, it too had split into two factions. On December 4, 1861, after the election of Abraham Lincoln and the fall of Fort Sumter, southern presbyteries separated from the Old School to form the Presbyterian Church in the Confederate States of America. In 1864 it joined with churches which had split from the New School. When the war ended in 1865 this new southern Presbyterian church changed its name to the Presbyterian Church in the United States.

Proslavery Biblical Arguments

Northern and southern churches were sharply divided, not only on cultural and political matters but on issues of biblical interpretation. Like current debates about the ordination of gays and lesbians, Christians did not agree about the proper interpretation of particular passages or about the principles that should be applied to the understanding of the Bible as a whole.

When the southern presbyteries broke away from the Old School, the first reason given for separation was the matter of fellowship, but the seceders quickly turned to their understanding of the Scriptures to support their action. They argued, first of all, that divorce was necessary to avoid the division that would naturally occur if politics obtruded into church courts and ministers and elders had to turn to acrimony, bitterness, and rancor. For them, it was more preferable to be apart during a time of war than to be together in debate and conflict in a period of peace.[20] Our Assembly, the southern Presbyterians argued, would present a mournful spectacle of strife, and the resulting conflict would leave the church lifeless and powerless, an easy prey to sectional divisions and the angry passions of its members. For them, the main cause of the separation was what they called "national peculiarities" that had broken the bonds of cordial fellowship.

The new Confederate Presbyterian Church charged that the break had been caused by Federalists proclaiming secession a crime and slavery a sin at an earlier meeting of the General Assembly. The separation was not created by the distance between sections of the country but by "the difference in the manners, customs and ways of thinking, the social, civil and political institutions of the people."[21]

Turning to the Scriptures, they argued that the only rule of judgment for them was found in the word of God, and they asked, "Do the Scriptures directly or indirectly condemn slavery as a sin? If they do not, the dispute is ended, for the Church, without forfeiting her character, dares not go beyond them."[22] Answering their own questions, using arguments that extend considerably past the mere use of proof texts and have, in fact, a very modern ring, the writers of the General Assembly statement developed a complex line of reasoning[23] that begins with the contention that the Bible nowhere denounces slavery, and that those who argue that it does merely "have gone to the Bible to confirm the crochets of their vain philosophy." Using an argument that sounds familiar to those accustomed to debates about the proper interpretation of Scripture in the twenty-first century, the General Assembly said that its opponents "have gone there determined to find a particular result, and the consequence is, that they leave with having made, instead of having interpreted, Scripture."[24]

In their view, slavery was "no new thing." It had existed for centuries and had been confirmed under every covenant of grace. The first church was inaugurated in the family of a slaveholder (Abraham, the father of all nations and the one to whom God first gave the covenant, Gen. 11:27–17:27) and the seal of circumcision was affixed to both slave and free. God continues to sanction slavery in the first tablet of the Ten Commandments, and it is found again in the churches "founded by the Apostles under the plenary inspiration of the Holy Ghost." These facts, they maintained, are utterly amazing if slavery is the enormous sin their northern enemies claimed it to be.

What is more, the statement continued, it is not possible to use Jesus' Golden Rule to condemn slavery. Arguing that all parts of the Bible have to say and mean the same thing if any part is to stand, those desiring separation wrote that it is impossible to contend that some sections of Scripture condone slavery and that others deny it without making Scripture inconsistent with itself. If slavery is condoned in some parts of the Bible, how could the Golden Rule say that it violated the law of love for one person to own another?

> . . . The law of love is simply the inculcation of universal equity; it implies nothing as to the existence of various ranks and gradations in society. The interpretation which makes it repudiate slavery would make it equally repudiate all social, civil and political inequities. . . . It condemns slavery, therefore, only upon the supposition that slavery is a sinful relation—that is, he who extracts the prohibition of slavery from the Golden Rule begs the very point in dispute.[25]

The PCCSA concluded, in a statement remarkable for its understatement, considering the fact that the war had already officially begun, that before secession the Presbyterian Church (i.e., the Old School) had advocated "a thoroughly scriptural policy in relation to *this delicate question* [emphasis added]," a policy that was set aside by the North when it declared slavery to be a sin.[26] Their final argument, one that all Christians in any age would like to be able to make about their own positions, claimed that their views were totally synchronous with the will of God as revealed in the Scriptures:

> We have assumed no new attitude. We stand exactly where the Church of God has always stood—from Abraham to Moses, from Moses to Christ, from Christ to the Reformers, and from the Reformers to ourselves. We stand upon the foundation of the Prophets and Apostles, Jesus Christ himself being the chief corner-stone. . . .[27]
>
> We are not ashamed to confess that we are intensely Presbyterian. We embrace all other denominations in the arms of Christian fellowship and love, but our own scheme of government we humbly believe to be according to the pattern shown in the Mount, and, by God's grace, we propose to put its efficiency to the test.[28]

Other scriptural arguments in favor of slavery that had been developed in preceding years remained implied or unsaid in the first statement of the PCCSA General Assembly, but they are also worth noting.[29]

1. Slavery was of divine origin and was entirely consistent with the laws of nature. The same creative order that keeps the planets in their orbits subjects black people to the will of white people. They are as bound to that order as the moons of Jupiter are bound to their orbit.

2. The New Testament supports the concept of slavery by ordering the obedience of slaves (Col. 3:22–25; Eph. 6:5–9; 1 Tim. 6:1–2; Titus 2:9–10; 1 Pet. 2:18–25), and Paul commands in the letter to Philemon that runaway slaves must return to their masters.

3. The book of Genesis (9:20–27) shows that blacks are inferior because they are descended from Ham, the son who shamed his father Noah (by observing his nakedness). Since Ham was "the father of Canaan," the degrading characteristics found in him are found in slaves even to the present day. Blacks were condemned to slavery because of their basic nature, a curse of servitude meant by God to be observed for all time

4. Biblical passages that call for the separation of church and state, especially those in Rom. 13 and in Jesus' teaching about giving to Caesar what is Caesar's (Mark 12:13–17; Matt. 22:15–22; Luke 20:20–26), demonstrate that the church has no right to modify government for the state. The state is a natural institute; the church is supernatural. Although it is possible for a collision to occur between the two, especially if there are wicked laws (the church then has a right to petition that they be repealed), this seldom happens: "Among a Christian people there is little difference of opinion as to the radical distinctions of right and wrong. The only serious danger is where moral duty is conditioned upon a political question."[30]

Abolitionist Biblical Arguments

So ran the arguments of those who thought that the Bible supports slavery. But what was the interpretative position of those who worked for slavery's abolition? Theodore Weld's assertions in his book *The Bible against Slavery* (published in 1864) are representative.[31] He argues from general principles of biblical interpretation, the law of love in the Old Testament, the teachings of Jesus, the absolute significance of justice before God, the nature of God's creative purpose, the central importance of the Golden Rule, and a sense of general human decency.

Weld's book was based on years of writing and speaking in favor of the abolition of slavery, and in the preface he admits that it is written with the hope that through the blessing of God the United States will be freed from the blight of slavery. Those who use the Bible to support slavery, he contends, have a false premise. In language that is apocalyptic, poetic, and passionate, he declares, "Slavery seeks refuge in the Bible only in the last extremity. It seizes the horns of the altar in desperation, rushing from the terror of the avenger's arm."[32] "[Slavery's asylum is] its sepulchre; its city of refuge, the city of destruction. It flies from the light into the sun; from heat into devouring fire; and from the voice of God into the thickest of His thunders."[33]

In Weld's opinion, the main argument against slavery involves a fundamental question of human rights. American slavery is guilty of reducing people into property, converting persons into things, turning immortality into merchandise.[34] Slavery does not rob a man of his privileges but of himself. It does not load him with burdens, but makes him a beast of burden.[35]

The Ten Commandments, Weld suggests, do not support slavery. They show that it is against God's law to take away from another what belongs to him. Slavery breaks this law by taking what human beings all have in common to themselves, namely, the title to themselves: "If one man's title is valid, all are valid. If one is worthless, all are." To take from a man his earnings violates the eighth commandment, but to take the earner himself compounds the sin; it is a matter of life-long theft.[36]

Weld examines several critical biblical passages. In Gen. 1:26–28 he turns to the concept of the image of God. Human beings are made in the image of God and should all be respected as such. Psalm 8:5–6 demonstrates that people are made a little lower than angels. God crowned them with glory and honor and gave them dominion over the work of their own hands.[37] In many cases where slavery is mentioned in the Bible, he contends, people were not forced into slavery but became servants of their own accord. Often they were paid for their work (Jer. 22:13).[38]

In his discussion of the concept of love of neighbor, Weld gives a broad definition of the word "neighbor." Examining Lev. 19:18 and related texts (Deut. 22:26; Prov. 25:8; Exod. 20:16), he convincingly argues that a neighbor is "anyone with whom we have to do," even a stranger. How, he asks, is it loving neighbors to make them work without pay, to rob them of their food and clothing? In an appendix, he considers pertinent New Testament texts by attaching, with approval, an address issued by the Presbyterian Synod of Kentucky in 1835 where it is argued that no matter how kindly a master may be to slaves, it is a violation of the Golden Rule to own them in the first place. Certainly it is not the way we would want to be treated or want our children to be treated: "We have received the command, 'Love thy neighbor as thyself,' and we are conscious that we are violating the whole spirit as well as the letter of this precept, when, for our own trifling pecuniary gain, we keep a whole race sunk in ignorance and pain."[39]

It is illegitimate, he continues, to argue from Gen. 9:25 and the mark of Canaan that blacks are cursed by God. It is the *vade mecum* of slaveholders, "a pocket-piece for sudden occasion, a keepsake to dote over, a charm to spell-bind opposition," but it is a lie. It is not clear, he points out, that Ham is the progenitor of all the African nations. It is not just to argue that a prophecy to one people justifies its infliction on another. "Cursed be Canaan" is but a mocking lullaby to unquiet tossings.[40] His disgust for those who use the Bible to support slavery is summarized in a harsh judgement: "The Bible defences thrown around slavery by professed ministers of the Gospel do so torture common sense, Scripture, and historical facts, it were hard to tell whether absurdity, fatuity, ignorance or blasphemy predominates, in the compound."[41]

Following the beginning of the war in 1861, the General Assembly of the New School adopted a resolution in support of the Union. In 1862 it issued a scathing indictment of slavery, calling it the main root of the conflict. After the declaration of the Emancipation Proclamation in 1863, it passed a resolution of joy that the yoke of oppression had been broken. In the same year, the United Presbyterian Church began work with black refugees behind the Union lines in Tennessee to help them find homes, clothing, food, health care, and education. In 1864 the General Assembly (Old School) initiated an investigation to look into mission for slaves and established a Committee for the Education of Freedmen. The two churches united their work in 1865 with a cooperative General Assembly Committee on Freedmen.[42]

Apartheid and the Bible

Although there was considerable change in the way Christian scholars interpreted the Bible after the Civil War, especially with the advance of the use of the historical-critical method, it may not be surprising that the discussion of human rights in relation to the Scriptures did not see much improvement or change. In fact, many biblical passages were interpreted in nearly the same way in support of the oppressive system of apartheid in South Africa.

Churches that supported apartheid frequently turned to texts utilized in the arguments of proslavery factions in the United States, especially those dealing with the order of creation (Gen. 1), the separation of the peoples in the time of Noah (Gen. 9:26–27), and the story of the tower of Babel (Gen. 11: 1–9). Interpreting these passages as literal history, a report published in 1975 by the largest South African white church (Dutch Reformed) contended that the sin of the people at the tower of Babel was in defying God's command given at creation and repeated to Noah that human beings were supposed to divide into different nations with separate languages and cultures.[43] The concept of diversity became the building block, therefore, for an ideology of separatism and racism.

The 1975 report also turned to Pentecost to buttress its arguments. The story of the giving of the Holy Spirit in Acts 2, it was argued, demonstrates that it is God's will that every person should learn the gospel in his or her own language. This passage confirms the principle that cultural identities, linguistic barriers, and the distinctiveness of groups of people is what God intended for the church. Turning to Acts 17:26, the Dutch Reformed Church asserted that God gave the nations one ancestor (Abraham) and established national identities and boundaries as part of the purpose determined at creation.

The concepts and ideologies found in this report were not created, of course, just prior to 1975. They were based on a clear history and tradition of interpretation of the Scriptures, what one scholar refers to as "the Apartheid Bible."[44] As J. A. Loubser points out, in the 1930s Afrikaners had ironically used the theme of the Exodus to support their own version of racism. Considering themselves to be called by God as the people of Israel were (Deut. 14:2), they argued that it was God who sent them into the interior of Africa as Voortrekkers to claim the land on God's behalf.[45] Around 1935 and thereafter, furthermore, a new philosophy was developed to provide a theological justification for apartheid. Loosely based on the teachings of John Calvin and referred to as "neo-Calvinism," it argued that the new state should not be founded on concepts of equality and liberal notions of democracy but on God's ordinances in creation. Since God had determined different colors of skin and different nations, it was the duty of God's elect to maintain that differentiation.[46] During World War II many Afrikaners expressed sympathy with the principles of the Nazi government and began to advocate the concept of racial purity in South Africa that found expression in oppressive marriage and sex laws.

Responses by Those Opposed to Apartheid

Loubser points to a number of major critiques of the theology behind apartheid.

1. Apartheid theology did not come from correct biblical interpretations but from the ideas of nationalism that developed in the romantic period of the eighteenth century.

2. The racial theories of apartheid, having alarming similarities to those of Nazi Germany, found their origins in an incorrect response to Darwin's theories of evolution and the concept of the survival of the fittest.

3. In hermeneutics, apartheid theology had little in common with Reformed principles of "scripture alone" and "Christ alone," but was reminiscent of the theories of natural law.[47] Critics also said that supporters of apartheid were using the Bible selectively as a kind of proof text. Responding to the 1975 report, Willem Vorster argued that

> the report is the result of a history of uncritical hermeneutics, a hermeneutics of acceptance in which the relevance of the Bible is not questioned but simply accepted and confessed. . . . The argumentation of the report runs in a vicious circle. It starts with an ideology which is introduced into Scripture and in the end it becomes an ideology based on Scripture. We do not need the Bible for this purpose. Common knowledge should suffice to judge the credibility of our decisions on human relations.[48]

Speaking of the necessity of using modern methods of biblical criticism, Vorster challenges proponents of apartheid to interpret the Bible in accordance with recognized principles of Reformed, scientific, and hermeneutical criticism. The Scriptures must not be used "biblistically" but interpreted in their own contexts and in the context of the entire history of salvation.[49]

One of the most powerful responses to apartheid theology came in 1985 when more than fifty black pastors and theologians from the townships around Johannesburg developed a confessional document commenting on the current racial crisis in South Africa. Reflecting on "the situation of death in our country," the participants called for "an alternative biblical and theological model that will in turn lead to forms of activity that will make a real difference to the future of our country." The Kairos Document[50] (the Greek word for time is *kairos*) opened with a strong challenge:

> The time has come. The moment of truth has arrived. South Africa has been plunged into a crisis that is shaking the foundations and there is every indication that the crisis has only just begun and that it will deepen and become

even more threatening in the months to come. It is the *KAIROS* or moment of truth not only for apartheid but also for the Church.

Noting that the church in South Africa stood divided about the way the Bible should be interpreted and society should be understood, the Kairos Document called for a reevaluation of theories of "state theology," "church theology," and "prophetic theology" that have led to oppression and death. It challenged the South African government's interpretation of Rom. 13 that merely serves as a "theological justification of the status quo with its racism, capitalism and totalitarianism. It blesses injustice, canonizes the will of the powerful and reduces the poor to passivity, obedience and apathy."

The Kairos Document called for change in the theology of the "English-speaking churches," which do not represent the majority of Africans. The document stated that the plea of these churches for reconciliation must be denied because in a state oppressed by apartheid, reconcilement and the desire to look at all sides of an issue can only lead to a compromise with evil, injustice, and sin. Reconciliation, forgiveness, and negotiation was deemed impossible without repentance on the part of the apartheid regime. What is needed, the document concluded, is a response from Christians that is biblical, spiritual, pastoral, and above all, prophetic, which demands a "reading of the signs of the times" (Matt. 16:3) through social analysis, an understanding of the description of oppression in the Bible, and a recognition of the use of tyranny in the Christian tradition. The South African government, by using apartheid to oppress God's people, and by becoming the enemy of the people, had become God's enemy. Both oppressor and oppressed must look to God for signs of hope as Christians are called to participate "in the struggle for liberation and a just society." The church must support consumer boycotts and "stayaways" as it moves from "a mere 'ambulance ministry' to one of involvement and participation."

> The Church of Jesus Christ is not called to be a bastion of caution and moderation. The Church should challenge, inspire and motivate people. It has a message of the cross that inspires us to make sacrifices for justice and liberation. It has a message of hope that challenges us to wake up and to act with hope and confidence. The Church must preach this message not only in words and sermons and statements but also through its actions, programmes, campaigns and divine services.

The theologians and pastors who signed the document urged churches around the world to provide support to prevent the loss of life that was spreading across the country.[51]

Reformed and Presbyterian Responses

Many churches had already provided powerful support in previous years and continued to do so after the publication of the Kairos Document. A brief chronology outlines some of the decisive actions:

1. As early as 1965 (and reiterated in 1981), the United Presbyterian Church in the U.S.A. declared that apartheid is theologically and morally indefensible: "Apartheid is gravely inimical to the present and future life, work, and witness of the Christian church because its ruthless deeds are blasphemously perpetrated in the name of Christ."[52]
2. In statements in 1966 at the world conference on Church in Society in Geneva, Switzerland, and with the launching of the Programme to Combat Racism in 1969, the World Council of Churches also began to challenge apartheid directly.[53]
3. The Presbyterian Church in the U.S. and the United Presbyterian Church addressed the situation some thirteen times between 1960 and 1985, and in 1981 and 1982 the General Assemblies of both churches adopted comprehensive statements on South Africa and Namibia, calling for a basic policy of "seeking peaceful but radical structural change, eliminating the apartheid system, and accomplishing independence for Namibia."[54]
4. Basing its support on previous declarations issued by the Assemblies of both the Presbyterian Church in the U.S. and the United Presbyterian Church, the 195th General Assembly (1983) of the Presbyterian Church (U.S.A.) reaffirmed its condemnation of apartheid and voted to sustain the action of the World Alliance of Reformed Churches that declared "that apartheid . . . is a sin, and that moral and theological justification of it is a travesty of the Gospel, and in its persistent disobedience to the Word of God, a theological heresy."[55]
5. In 1985 the reunited church spent considerable time expressing concern for the worsening situation in South Africa and included carefully researched studies of the background of the crisis. The General Assembly moved to affirm the action of the World Alliance of Reformed Churches to suspend two white Reformed churches from its membership (the Nederduitse Gereformeerde Kerk and the Nederduitse Hervormde Kerk). At that meeting, it included intercessory prayers for all of the people of South Africa in general and for the Rev. Allen Boesak and his wife Dorothy in particular. In 1985 the General Assembly initiated a policy of divestment of the stocks of companies doing business in South Africa, beginning with Fluor, Mobil, Newmont Mining, and Texaco.[56] Presbyterians were by no means in agreement about the implementation of this strategy,[57] but the debate about divestment had been going on for more than twenty-five years, and the General Assembly finally supported the

contention that the presence of foreign corporations in South Africa bolstered apartheid and that withdrawal or radical changes were required for a peaceful transition to democracy.

6. In 1987, at the time of its bicentennial celebration, the General Assembly received information that divestment was having a powerful impact on the situation in South Africa, forcing many companies to leave the country. The Rev. Leon Sullivan, author of a code of conduct for U.S. companies in South Africa, urged that additional pressure should be exerted for more corporations to withdraw. The General Assembly concurred with committee recommendations that the securities of Citicorp, Control Data, Ford Motor Company, General Motors, and Unisys be subject to divestment or proscription according to the policy adopted in 1985.[58]

The employment of the strategy of divestment may seem like a radical response to the biblical command to let God's people go, but it clearly recognizes that there must be a connection between our hearts and our wallets. If our souls are where our money is, we need to acknowledge that economics is a matter of faith. On a personal note, I recall preaching a sermon when I was the pastor of the First Presbyterian Church in Plattsburgh, New York, against apartheid as a hateful regime that denies the basic principles of the gospel. One of our members, a wealthy businessman whose global company had investments in South Africa, invited me to visit him at his home during the next week. He took the opportunity to tell me that he was leaving the church because my sermon offended him. All I could say, looking him in the eye, was, "I am sorry that my preaching against apartheid did not offend you sooner."

Divestment put enormous pressure on the racist South African government and on companies who made a profit on the backs of exploited workers. When churches withdrew investments in companies in South Africa, it represented a large percentage of the $250 million of U.S. holdings in that country. Before South Africans obtained their freedom in 1994, Mobil had sold all of its assets there (1989) and banks stopped making loans to the South African government, so it was eventually unable to repay its international debt. By 1987, U.S. religious bodies had withdrawn more than $125 million in accounts from Citibank alone.[59] As Desmond Tutu put it, "The Church that is in solidarity with the poor can never be a Wealthy Church. It must sell all in a sense to follow the Master. It must sit loosely to the things of this world, using its wealth and resources for the sake of the least of Christ's brethren."[60]

Presbyterians can be proud of the way in which the church worked with other Christians and human rights groups throughout the world to hasten the downfall of apartheid. We need to remember, of course, that most of our contribution was through theological and policy statements or the application of economic pressure.[61] Many men, women, and children paid a much higher price and were willing to give their lives to end apartheid. Speaking of the terrible years he had to spend in prison, Nelson Mandela writes, "I am no more virtuous or self-sacrificing than the next man, but I found that I could not even enjoy the poor and limited freedoms I was allowed when I knew that my people were not free. Freedom is indivisible; the chains on any one of my people were the chains on all of them, the chains on all of my people were chains on me."[62]

Segregation, Civil Rights, and the Bible

Although it may seem repetitive to review Bible texts and theological arguments used to support segregation in the United States in the twentieth century after having explored their use in support of slavery and apartheid, it is necessary to do so in order to help dispel the mistaken notion that modern sophistication or the use of the principles of higher biblical criticism are alone sufficient to prevent racism in contemporary society. In fact, a brief examination of prosegregation arguments in the 1940s through the 1980s demonstrates that the same biblical texts were brought out again to justify prejudice and oppression.

Genesis 9:24–27 was used, for example, to prove that blacks are cursed by God and not worthy to live or work with whites. Genesis 11 and the story of the tower of Babel were connected with the account of the giving of the Holy Spirit in Acts 2 to buttress the argument that it is God's will that different human beings should be separate and apart. Acts 17:26 supported the thesis that it was God's intention to separate the nations (and peoples) of the earth by clear boundaries.[63] Proponents of segregation argued again that Rom. 13:1–7 calls for absolute obedience to all government authorities, whether they are oppressive or not.

In the 1950s, attacks on the NAACP (National Association for the Advancement of Colored People) were reminiscent of the vicious criticisms leveled at proponents of the antislavery movement some one hundred years before as segregationists charged that international communist plots were behind liberal organizations that supported integration.[64]

Christians who supported racial equality, on the other hand, took a very different view of the biblical texts in question. The curse of Ham, they argued, was not a blight on Africans or all black people in general. The sons of Noah were not to be regarded as progenitors of all men and women of color. Even though the etiology of the story marks the Canaanites as Israel's enemies, they are not to be equated with any modern national entity. Although it is true that God separates the people in the tower of Babel narrative, it happens not because God wills it but because of human sin. Acts 2, rather than showing that God wants people apart, demonstrates just the opposite. It reverses any negative effects of the dispersion of the nations by calling all people back into one family of Christ.[65]

Supporters of the civil and spiritual rights of blacks demonstrated, furthermore, that Rom. 13 cannot be used to demand the uncritical support of all government actions. Even if Christians were forced to submit to the emperor in Paul's day, believers in the twentieth century should know that if governments can be elected, they can also be removed from office. Since the power that government possesses comes from God, authorities only keep that power as long as their actions reflect the authority of God. When secular leaders are not acting according to God's will, for the general good (Rom. 13:4, 6), or on behalf of the oppressed and poor whom God particularly loves (Ps. 72), Christians have a right and an obligation to say "no" and to participate actively in the struggle for liberation and justice.[66]

Presbyterian Support for Civil Rights

When did Presbyterians begin to work for racial equality in the United States in an active way? The Confession of 1967 affirms that God has created the peoples of the earth to be one universal family and that through the love of Christ all barriers between brothers and sisters are broken down: "Therefore, the church labors for the abolition of all racial discrimination and ministers to those injured by it. Congregations, individuals, or groups of Christians who exclude, dominate, or patronize their fellowmen, however subtly, resist the Spirit of God and bring contempt on the faith which they profess" (C-9.44). Recognizable movement toward integration began some thirty-five years earlier, however, when Dr. Josiah W. Holley, a black pastor, was elected in 1932 to one of the official boards of the church.[67] Six years later, Dr. A. B. McCoy became the first black to serve as an executive of a board, being elected secretary of the Department of Work with Colored People. In 1944 the General Assembly of the UPCUSA issued the first of many strong policy statements, this one declaring that discrimination or segregation on the basis of race is "undemocratic and unchristian" and pledging to work for the creation of "a non-segregated Church in a non-segregated society." The next General Assembly went even further and called upon members belonging to organizations still practicing racial discrimination to work to eliminate such practices. In 1947, the year when Jackie Robinson joined the Brooklyn Dodgers and one year before President Truman ordered the integration of the Armed Forces, the Committee on Racial and Cultural Relations was directed to recommend policies to make the practice of the church in all areas conform to the standard of "brotherhood" taught by Jesus. That same year, the PCUS Assembly condemned all organizations or individuals attempting to hinder minorities "in the exercise of their civil rights or deny [them] such rights on the basis of race, creed, or color."[68]

In 1952 the statement made in 1944 was reaffirmed, and the UPCUSA General Assembly called upon Congress to eliminate segregation in the nation's capital. The PCUS Assembly similarly urged its legislators to support civil rights legislation, and in 1953 reaffirmed its opposition to the exploitation of racial prejudice for political purposes. In 1955, one year after the U.S. Supreme Court ruled that racial discrimination in public schools was a violation of the fourteenth amendment, the UPCUSA called for "Operation Desegregation" in all of its congregations, institutions, and communities. The year that President Eisenhower signed a bill reasserting the voting rights of all Americans (1957), the PCUS spoke out against poll taxes and literary tests. The UPCUSA General Assembly endorsed equal voting rights, open occupancy, and fair housing legislation in 1958.

In the 1960s, as the nation entered into the most impassioned debates about civil rights, when violence struck the cities of Newark, Detroit, and Los Angeles, when the marches began on Selma and other cities, when some of our best political and spiritual leaders were lost to assassins' bullets, the church began to move more boldly and powerfully in support of the rights of all racial and ethnic groups. 1963 stands out in particular because in that year the 175th General Assembly of the United Presbyterian Church created the Commission on Religion and Race (CORAR) and requested it "to design a comprehensive and coordinated strategy" for the church's approach to race relations.[69] Over the years its recommendations provided a powerful impetus in the stand against discrimination. In 1964, with the Rev. Gayraud S. Wilmore Jr. as its executive director, CORAR reported that it would provide more leadership to bring the church's practices into line with its previous pronouncements, especially in reference to the employment of "Negroes" in church agencies and the use of minority groups as suppliers of goods and services. A report entitled "The Civil Rights Movement in the Light of Christian Teaching" was approved by the PCUS Assembly. This report addressed the problems of racism in the South and called for justice for all minority groups. In 1966 CORAR reported further on the development of a program designed to support judicatories as they created projects to combat racism and provide backing for voter registration projects, antipoverty programs in the South, and community organizations working for civil rights across the country. With the establishment of the Fund for Freedom (a churchwide offering for civil rights), more than $300,000 was raised in two years to help finance both types of programs. In a powerful closing statement, the report concluded,

> The United Presbyterian Church, by pronouncement and policy statement and by the creation of the Commission on Religion and Race, has declared to the American people that the imperative of the gospel impels it to reshape every aspect of its life to reflect the oneness and equality of all men in Jesus Christ. As the Church uproots every vestige of conscious and unconscious racism from its own life it will be that more enabled to eliminate it from the social order. The United Presbyterian Church has entered upon that path and will not turn back.[70]

In 1965, in recognition of the tenth anniversary of the historic ruling of the Supreme Court, the Standing Committee on Church and Society presented the following statement to the General Assembly:

> It is now time for the Church to go to "the heart of the matter," to address itself to the sinful blindness of the human spirit that, added to the structural rigidities of social, economic, and political arrangements, perpetuates hatred and recrimination, segregation and discrimination, estrangement and distrust, between white and nonwhite. . . . Racism is basically the denial of the humanity of all other races but one's own, the deliberate or unconscious assumption that a human being's worth is conditioned by his racial deriva-tion.... The New Testament, although it has been quoted with facility to jus-tify the position of both the "segregationist" and the "integrationist," is clear at this point when interpreted not by texts but as a whole within the Reformed tradition. The "wall of separation" [Eph. 2:14] that divides and estranges men from each other and from God has been totally broken down for those that believe the gospel. God was in Christ reconciling "the world" to himself [2 Cor. 5:19], not just certain races of the world.[71]

With these principles and others in mind, the General Assembly was urged to repudiate racism and all its manifestations in the life of the church and its members as blasphemy and contrary to the love of God revealed in Jesus Christ. All members, judicatories, boards, and agencies were directed to con-tinue and to intensify actions to eliminate patterns of segregation in church and in society, to work with others for the nullification of laws prohibiting interracial marriage, and to support the revision of federal law to make it pos-sible to prosecute (in federal courts) those responsible for the deaths of oth-ers by conspiring to deprive them of their civil rights.[72]

In 1983, when the northern and southern branches of the church were finally reunited, the PC(USA) officially endorsed the continuing work of the Council on Church and Race (the new name given to CORAR in 1981), paying special attention to a document entitled "A Comprehensive Strategy on Racial Justice in the 1980's."[73] The report, which now belonged to the whole denomination, called for a battle against racism in every aspect of American life and was used to define Presbyterian actions for the next two decades:

> As bearers of the Reformed and reforming tradition, . . . Presbyterians understand ministry to be everybody's business. As a denomination striving to understand the Kingdom of God to be incarnate in the Prince of Peace, who is both Lord of Life and Servant of Justice as the body of Christ, we know that racial justice is every Presbyterian's business. As persons aware of the pervasiveness of racism within our world, we realize that racial justice is every ministry's business.[74]

Prospects: How Can the Text Be Rightly Used in the Future?

An examination of the different responses of Presbyterians and other Christians within the Reformed tradition to persistent threats of slavery, separatism, and racism over three centuries provides valuable and fascinating insights into the way believers interpret the Bible during crises. It also raises a critical question about the future. How will believers understand the Scriptures if human rights are in danger in the decades ahead?

Although it is tempting to assume that the sophistication of modern thought, the power of democratic reform, openness of communication in the so-called Information Age, and more advanced methods of Bible study will prevent human rights violations in the years to come, a few considerations demonstrate how naive such hope may be. Historical analogies imply that struggles for freedom often require decades of political and theological debate and that issues often are not resolved until violence forces them to conclusion. How much patience will Presbyterians be required to exercise in regard to theological and social concerns that will surely be faced in the future? Are we missing the lessons of history when we try to resolve knotty human and theological problems in a hurry? Will debates on human rights and questions about sexual preference and church office also drag out for decades while believers examine and reexamine the Bible and Christian theology? Will the matter finally be decided only when the church experiences another fracture? Or will we have the wisdom to find a better way?

Certainly modern methods of Bible study, our knowledge of biblical languages, and increasing archaeological data will all help us avoid the mistakes of our forebears. But will these advantages be enough? The Presbyterians who used the Scriptures to argue for slavery and the Christians who utilized the same passages to support apartheid and segregation were not all biblically or theologically illiterate. Their arguments, refined somewhat, might still be attractive to people in years to come. The methodologies they used, under modern guise, are still utilized by some interpreters and churches today. What is more, it is not difficult to see how it is possible to misuse and misinterpret the Bible in the service of our own prejudices if we merely cite individual texts to support preconceived notions. If we do not go beyond the lessons gleaned from single passages to broader issues of Christian love, a more universal definition of who the neighbor is, and a more comprehensive understanding of God's intention to love all the people and nations of the world as children of God, and if we do not acknowledge the certainty that God wills justice for the marginalized and the oppressed, we may find ourselves making worse mistakes in the future than believers did in the past.

Will we have the passion to struggle for freedom for those who are under the control of modern Pharaohs? The question may reduce itself simply to demanding that they let God's children go and using all peaceful means to make sure that they do. As Desmond Tutu says, the Bible teaches that each human being is truly a child of God, invested with infinite value and not some arbitrarily chosen biological attribute. Every human being is made in God's image (Gen. 1:26), and any system that claims that a person only qualifies for freedom and power because of skin color or ethnic antecedents is guilty of opposition to God's creative purpose. As Tutu asserts, "That is clearly at variance with the teaching of the Bible and the teaching of our Lord and Saviour Jesus Christ. Hence the church's criticisms that your . . . policies are not only unjust and oppressive. They are positively unbiblical, unchristian, immoral and evil."[75]

A review of the recent past indicates that the battle against racism and oppression is far from over. The severe beating of Rodney King in Los Angeles, racial profiling of minorities by police in New Jersey and other states and local municipalities, race riots in Cincinnati, the continuing isolation of Native Americans in the United States, economic exploitation of immigrant workers in this country (and laborers in third world countries), racial wars still being fought in parts of Africa and Asia, and the horrible spectacle of slave ships carrying African children from Benin, Togo, Mali, Senegal, and Guinea[76] to lives of hardship and agony remind us that what earlier generations called the "blasphemy" of racism is still part of our world. The refusal of the United States to participate in the World Conference against Racism that was held in South Africa in August 2001 demonstrates how much human rights definitions are still determined by political considerations. The bitter debates that followed that meeting indicate how volatile questions are about paying reparations to the descendants of African slaves or how difficult it is to define the nature of racism in Israel, Palestine, and other parts of the Middle East. Will the church learn from the past and use all forms of theological, political, and economic power to stop human suffering, or will it merely continue in discussion and debate?[77] As the poet Vachel Lindsay put it,

> This is the sin against the Holy Ghost:
> To speak of bloody power as right divine,
> And call on God to guard each vile chief's house,
> And for such chiefs, turn men to wolves and swine.
> . . . .
> This is the sin against the Holy Ghost:
> This is the sin no purging can atone:
> To send forth rapine in the name of Christ:
> To set the face and make the heart a stone.[78]

Questions for Study and Reflection
1. Do you see any similarities between current debates about the Bible and social issues today and those that took place prior to the Civil War? How are these debates different?
2. Why do you think that some people deny the basic personhood of those who are different from them?
3. If all the people of the world really are children of God, how should we treat them?

Chapter 6

No Longer Male and Female
Galatians 3:28–29

There is no longer Jew or Greek, there is no longer slave or free, there is no longer male and female; for all of you are one in Christ Jesus. And if you belong to Christ, then you are Abraham's offspring, heirs according to the promise.

Centrality of the Text

*S*he is the best-known member of the Presbyterian church she attended. The sanctuary continues to echo with her words as members remember that she once worshiped among them. Her great-great-grandchildren visit her hometown to see plays performed in her honor and to stop by the corner of Main and Market where she was born when her father was the county judge. Two blocks away on William Street, the house still stands where she and Susan B. Anthony boarded with Mrs. Henry in 1884 to write the third volume of *The History of Woman Suffrage.*[1]

Those of us who are members of the PC(USA) can be proud to remember that a woman like Elizabeth Cady Stanton was raised a Presbyterian in Johnstown, New York, even if she rebelled at an early age against some of the teachings of the church. On the day in 1840 when she was secretly married in the Presbyterian sanctuary to Henry Stanton, a leader in the abolitionist movement, Elizabeth boldly told the Rev. Hugh Marie that she would not repeat the vow "to love, honor, and obey." It was impossible, she said, to obey someone with whom she was supposed to be equal.[2]

After the couple returned from a working honeymoon in London and the World Anti-Slavery Convention (where Elizabeth worked with Lucretia Mott and others to win women the right to speak for themselves at the conference), they settled for a short time in Johnstown. At first she was happy to be back home, and she invested herself in teaching Sunday school at her church. When members of the congregation refused to allow black children to enter the sanctuary during a special procession, however, she resigned in disgust and began a period in her life in which she took the liberty to examine her faith critically.

Her most famous religious work, *The Woman's Bible* (published in 1898), directly challenged a male-dominated church and, anticipating the work of feminist commentators some seventy or more years later, charged that the Bible had been used to keep women in their place, in civil and political degradation, and in an unequal position in the church.[3] Women were subordinated, she argued, not only by the way passages were interpreted in which women appeared but in the ones in which they were "prominent by exclusion." Working from the original Hebrew and Greek, Elizabeth Cady Stanton wrote with seven other women to provide a new translation and interpretation of key passages that influenced the way women were treated in the church and in society. She anticipated modern criticism by acknowledging the fact that women were victims, as were others, of interpretations that claim that all Bible passages say only one thing about a given subject:

> There are lofty examples of good and true men and women, all worthy our acceptance and imitation whose lustre cannot be dimmed by the false sentiments and vicious characters bound up in the same volume. The Bible cannot be accepted or rejected as a whole, its teachings are varied and its lessons differ widely from each other. In criticizing the peccadilloes of Sarah, Rebecca and Rachel, we would not shadow the virtues of Deborah, Huldah and Vashti. In criticizing the Mosaic code we should not question the wisdom of the golden rule and the fifth Commandment.[4]

Stanton's comments raise important questions. What kind of portrait has the Bible drawn of women? What are the positive and negative images it has portrayed? How have Presbyterians offered affirmations and/or betrayals, and what does the future portend for women in our church and in the Christian community as a whole?

The Text

Galatians 3:28 is a critical text for the proper understanding of the role of women in the church: "There is no longer Jew or Greek, there is no longer slave or free, there is no longer male and female; for all of you are one in Christ Jesus." Here Paul clearly states that women and men, as coheirs of salvation in Jesus Christ, are partners in ministry and sisters and brothers of Jesus Christ. Although it is likely that he came to this conclusion through some struggle and internal debate, if other comments he makes elsewhere are taken at face value (cf. 1 Cor. 11:1–16; 14:34–36), it is fair to say that in these verses his developed thoughts on the subject, the ones grounded on his most mature preaching of the gospel, are presented.[5]

Why is the Galatians passage so important? Paul's statement represents the first time that a clear declaration is made in a Christian document about the equality of men and women. What is more, as some commentators point out, the concept of unity in Christ in 3:28 is so powerful that it appears to be designed to challenge the church with social and political implications that are nearly revolutionary in scope and dimension.[6] Here Paul takes the three places where discrimination was most stringently enforced in the ancient world—in racial (or religious) relationships, in the institution of slavery, and in the role of women in society—and uses what was probably a preexisting baptismal formula to reinterpret them in light of God's plan for salvation in Christ and the Christian hope for the future. These verses have often been called "the Magna Charta of humanity." Even if Paul knew that all of these distinctions would not disappear in his own lifetime, it is clear that he hoped that they would ultimately count in the church of the future, where the most important thing would not be the status quo but the new creation.[7]

It may have taken some time for Paul to come to this stunning conclusion. His own mind may have been changed over the years by preaching the gospel and by the experience of working with women in the church. Indeed, his attitude in Galatians seems to approximate what we know about Jesus' attitude toward the presence of women in the ministry of the kingdom more closely than his earlier writings do.

Despite the difficulty scholars have in determining the precise outline of Jesus' life, or the exact contours of his sayings or ministry (the question of the historical Jesus), even a cursory glance at the gospels shows that spiritual women influenced his life profoundly and that they played pivotal roles in the development of his own mission:

- Elizabeth, his mother's cousin, believed the impossible promise of God in her old age (Luke 1:39–45);
- Mary, his mother, accepted the angel's message and looked forward to the time when God would fill the hungry with good things and send the rich away empty (Luke 1:46–56);
- Anna, a prophet, praised God in the temple and looked for the redemption of Israel (Luke 2:36–40).

Jesus healed women frequently, conversed with them regularly, accepted them as friends, and encouraged them to follow him and minister to him. The group that watched him die on the cross was mostly women, and the only people who received God's good news of resurrection at first were female family members and followers. According to John, the first person to see the risen Lord was Mary (John 20:11–18), and in Acts, women were present in the upper room at the first meeting of the disciples after Jesus returned to heaven (Acts 1:14). As Thomas John Carlisle wrote in one of his poems, women did much more than serve the kingdom in traditional ways:

> There may have been room
> in the upper room
> for women
> not primarily
> for preparing food
> or serving it
> but definitely
> for sharing at the table.[8]

In Paul's ministry, women played an increasingly prominent role as well. Mary, the mother of Mark, had a church meeting in her home in Jerusalem at a time when to do so could mean death (Acts 12:12). Her son later worked with Paul for a time (Acts 12:25; Col. 4:10; Phlm. 24). Lydia, the first convert in Europe, was a wealthy businesswoman who specialized in the sale of expensive purple cloth and led her whole household into the church (Acts 16:14–40). Priscilla, along with her husband Aquila, was an important leader in Corinth. They helped finance Paul's missionary journeys, had a church in their home, and risked their lives for him (Acts 18:1–2; Rom. 16:3; 1 Cor. 16:19; 2 Tim. 4:19). In Rom. 16, moreover, several women are mentioned as critical to Paul's ministry in the capital: Mary, Tryphaena and Tryphosa, Rufus's mother, Nereus's sister, Julia, and Olympas. Phoebe is commended as a deacon in the church (16:1), and Junia, a relative of Paul's who once did jail time with him, is listed as an apostle (16:7).[9]

> The stories point
> beyond themselves.
> They tell of women.
> They tell
> more than the tellers
> realized they told.
>
> And Jesus still
> opens the scriptures

to new treasures for us
beyond the bounds
of our perimeters.[10]

It is unfortunate that these primary texts about the role of women in ministry were often ignored by the church throughout its history in favor of those that seem to support subordination and patriarchy. It is even more tragic that in many conservative Christian circles today the negative texts still receive top priority. Women are forced to assume less powerful roles in the church and are dominated by their husbands in public and in private, presumably according to the authority of the word of God.

Common sense should rule out such interpretations, of course, when women play such a prominent role in every profession in modern life, but so should solid biblical interpretation. It is clear that many of the New Testament texts which patronize women illustrate what is meant in the Confession of 1967 when it says that the Scriptures, given under the guidance of the Holy Spirit, are nonetheless the words of human beings, "conditioned by the language, thought forms, and literary fashions of the places and times at which they were written. They reflect views of life, history, and the cosmos which were then current" (C-9.29).

First Corinthians 11:1–16 is a major case in point. In these verses, Paul clearly considers women to be subordinate to men in the church, based on social custom as he understands it. Nevertheless, even if his arguments were persuasive to members of the church in Corinth (obviously someone had a different viewpoint or he would not have brought up the matter in the first place), they are not to most Christians in the twenty-first century. His teaching that women must enter a church service with their heads covered, for example, reflects the social custom which demands that women demonstrate their modesty and inferiority by wearing a veil or scarf of some kind. Jewish custom asserted that women who had their heads uncovered were guilty of violating the order of creation in Gen. 1–3 (1 Cor. 11:7–12). Those who let their hair down were considered to be sexually loose, since such an act was only supposed to take place in the privacy of one's home, in the presence of one's husband.[11]

Perhaps 1 Cor. 11 reflects a historical situation in which Paul is worried about the reputation and public image of the new church. If Christians suddenly abandoned conservative public customs, he reasons, they would be accused of harming society, thus giving the church bad press. First Corinthians 11:17–34 indicates, furthermore, that chaos was threatening to undermine the sanctity of Corinthian worship and celebration of the Lord's Supper, and Paul proposes to reestablish order by limiting nontraditional behavior. Understanding the situation helps modern readers appreciate Paul's concerns, but it does not change the fact that his advice is no longer relevant to the church. His understanding of the order of creation is based on a faulty construction, since Gen. 1:27 clearly indicates that men are not superior to women there. Although restrictions about attire and hairstyle are still important in religious communities today (some branches of Islam), most contemporary Presbyterians would agree that the length of one's hair reflects nothing more than fashion and personal preference.

Another well-known passage in which the subordination of women is advocated also presents interpretative difficulties. In 1 Cor. 14:34–35 Paul asserts that women should remain silent in the church and ask their husbands at home if there is something they need to understand. Those who think that this passage is an original part of Paul's letter to the Corinthians often argue that it reflects the kind of situation described by a later writer in 1 Tim. 2:11–12 where women were believed to be embarrassing their husbands or church leaders by speaking up indiscriminately. Perhaps Paul is illustrating what he has already mentioned in 14:23–33, where he says that unbridled individualism and open discussion of the meaning of tongues is disruptive to worship: "Let two or three prophets speak, and let the others weigh what is said. If a revelation is made to someone else sitting nearby, let the first person be silent" (vv. 29–30).

Other commentators, however, do not see how Paul could have written the verses in question. In their opinion, 14:34–35 seems to be so completely out of context, in light of the previous discussion of spiritual gifts, and so out of keeping with Paul's comments in 11:5 where it is indicated that women did speak (pray and prophesy) during church services, that they are forced to conclude that Paul did not write these words at all. They are, these commentators say, an interpolation inserted by a later writer who wanted to make Paul's position even more conservative than it already was.[12] As Gordon D. Fee notes in his commentary on 1 Corinthians, "The exegesis of the text itself leads to the conclusion that it is not authentic. If so, then it is certainly not binding for Christians."[13] Clearly it cannot be applied to a church that calls its women to be equal partners in ministry as preachers and teachers all over the world.

A third passage that still serves the purpose of limiting the role of women in the church and at home is Eph. 5:21–33. In these verses, someone using Paul's name writes that women should "be subject" to their husbands, as they are to the Lord (either God or Christ). As Christ is head of the church, so the husband is the head of the wife. Although it may seem amazing, these verses still have a powerful influence on many conservative Christian families where it is believed that it violates God's word for the wife to argue with her husband or assume responsibility in the household. In many cases, it is women themselves who are the strongest advocate for this position, even in situations where the husband is totally incapable of taking care of himself, much less a wife and children.

In one church in which I served, a woman came to me for pastoral counseling because her husband was abusing her. When she went to her own pastor for advice (she was a member of a conservative Pentecostal church), he told her that her desire to change the relationship in her marriage was contrary to God's word in Ephesians. Not only was she disobeying her husband, the pastor said, she was also disobeying God. My point of view was very different. "What you need," I said, "is more than a new husband. How can you function if your husband, your pastor, and your God are all against you? What you need is a new marriage, a new church, and a new understanding of the Bible!" Although it was very difficult for her, she eventually jettisoned her former understanding of women, got a divorce from a husband who continued to abuse her physically and emotionally, and joined our church, where she found a new appreciation of women as partners in marriage and in Christ's service.

Because it has often been misunderstood, Eph. 5:21–33 has caused tremendous suffering in the church and in the lives of individual Christians. Although the passage clearly represents a patriarchal view of society prevalent in the first century, its more revolutionary aspects are often overlooked. At first glance it appears that the author is not challenging the prevalent view that all of society is arranged in a predictable hierarchy. Just as God is at the apex of authority in the universe, so the emperor is the head of all human rule. The governor in each Roman province was subject to the emperor, and the king (such as Herod) was subject to the governor. The king commanded local officials who ran the community and had power over individual citizens (all men). In the household, the eldest male or the husband had the same kind of power over all others who were required to take orders from him (women, children, and slaves; see Eph. 6:1–9).

In Eph. 5:21–33, however, the author makes a modest attempt to prevent the kind of abuse that might develop in such a family system. Verse 21 sets the tone: "Be subject to one another out of reverence for Christ." It is as if the author were saying, "Yes, it is true that the wife is subject to the husband in the world. That is the way of all things right now. But there is one slight difference for those who are church members. Even if the husband is the head of the wife, he has to treat his wife just as Christ treats him, and in many ways the old rules no longer apply." The revolutionary aspect comes in the comparison of the husband's behavior with that of the Lord's. Obviously, since Jesus died for all men and women and loves them with unlimited love, if the husband treated his wife the same way there would be no need for subjection. It is almost as if the author is saying, "Regardless of how society conceives the relationship between men and women, Christian husbands and wives are no longer free to continue that practice. You must love each other with the love of Christ." In such a case, it becomes immaterial who is the head and who is subject. Even if the writer had said, "Husbands, be subject to your wives as you are to the Lord. For the wife is the head of the husband just as Christ is the head of the church," it would still come out the same, because if both partners love as Christ loves, with generous, self-giving love, the marriage has already moved past the concept of domination to one of partnership and equality.

Other New Testament passages that have also served the purpose of denying women their rightful place in the church also deserve to be examined. In 1 Tim. 2:8–15, the author (Paul did not write the Pastoral Epistles) asserts that women should act modestly in the church: "Let a woman learn in silence with full submission. I permit no woman to teach or to have authority over a man; she is to keep silent. For Adam was formed first, then Eve; and Adam was not deceived, but the woman was deceived and became a transgressor." Somewhat similar restrictions are placed on women in the church in Titus 2:3–5, where it is argued that women who speak too much, or in an incorrect way, bring discredit to the gospel. These passages appear to reflect a position that is much more conservative than that found in the letter to the Galatians. Worried about questions of authority in the church, and anxious to preserve conservative religious and social traditions, the authors employ rabbinic interpretations of Gen. 3 that claim there is significance in the order in which Adam and Eve were created. With a kind of *cherchez la femme* attitude, the author of 1 Timothy blames sin on Eve, who took the forbidden fruit first ("From a woman sin had its beginning, and because of her we all die" [cited in Sir. 25:24]).

Although Jews and Christians have used similar theological arguments to restrain women for centuries, biblical scholars now demonstrate that such interpretations violate the Genesis text. As Walter Brueggemann says concerning the Genesis accounts of Adam and Eve, "Popular tradition concerning fall, 'apples and snakes,' is prone to focus this narrative around questions of sex and the evil wrought by sex." It is possible that the serpent and the mention of nakedness (Gen. 2:25; 3:7) are derived from sexual symbolism. "But to find in this any focus on sex or any linkage between sex and sin is not faithful to the narrative. Insofar as the text reflects on the relation of the sexes, its concern is with the political dynamics of power, control, and autonomy."[14]

Other New Testament texts central to the debate that have been used to deny women their proper role in the church could be explored, such as 1 Pet. 3:7, where women are referred to as "the weaker sex," or Rev. 17:5, where the Roman Empire is called "Babylon the great, mother of whores and of earth's abominations." Some Old Testament narratives depict women as true followers of God (the stories of Sarah, Rebekah, Deborah, Jael, Miriam, Esther, and the good wife in Prov. 31 to mention a few), whereas other texts offer mixed portrayals of Tamar (Gen. 38), Rahab (Josh. 2), or Jezebel (2 Kgs. 9:30–37; Rev. 2:20) in leadership roles.[15] Nevertheless, the examples given demonstrate that modern Christians need to do more than take the Gospels, the letters of Paul, and the Old Testament narratives at simple face value. Discerning readers also need to understand the backgrounds and histories of the texts, interpret them in light of their own unique historical circumstances, and be in dialogue with them. As Barbara Hall said many years ago in reference to the writings of Paul, we must do more than close our eyes and say that "Paul is not really so bad," or "Paul is complex and says different things." As Hall puts it, these are all true, "but Paul and the rest of the Bible offer us more than that—namely, some important things about how liberation and transformation of relationships occur concretely, and how we may lay hold of them."[16] The only way we can do that is to take all of the biblical texts seriously and be in conversation with them so that the Holy Spirit can direct us to the ones that reveal God's will for the church today.

Use in the Reformed Tradition and the Presbyterian Church

How were women regarded in the church during the period of the Reformation and the years that followed? The writings of John Calvin indicate that many of the biblical texts that portrayed women in a negative light continued to be lifted up. Even without knowing the details of the role of women in the churches that John Calvin directed, a great deal can be inferred about the practices he espoused by examining his *Institutes of the Christian Religion* and the commentaries he wrote. Clearly women were subordinate to men in the church in Geneva and were deliberately kept from assuming positions of power and authority.

When Calvin discusses the concept of sexual relationships, for example, it is clear that the only ramifications of the question that need to be considered, as far as he is concerned, are those that apply to men. Writing to the men in the church, he seems to lament the powerful influence that mothers and wives have on his readers: "Now, through the condition of our nature, and by the lust aroused after the Fall, we, except for those whom God has released through special grace, are doubly subject to women's society. Let each man, then, see what has been given to him" (2.8.42). If a man needs to marry, however, it is not a bad thing, since in this state of repose and convenience he is better prepared for Christian ministry, since "he may be more prompt and ready for all the duties of piety" (2.8.43).

Calvin makes it clear that ministry is a calling only for men and argues strongly against those who try to use biblical precedents to argue that women should be allowed to perform baptism. Such an act of ministry is a grave sin because it violates the rule of Christ that only extends the call to men (4.15.22). In a section of his commentary on 1 Corinthians in which he considers Gal. 3:28, he contends that Paul is not in favor of equality between men and women in civic or church duties. The distinction decried in that verse is only spiritual in nature and does not apply to politics or ministry.[17] In his opinion, 1 Cor. 11:9 demonstrates that woman is inferior to man and mainly functions as his glory, since "the woman was created for the express purpose of greatly enriching the man's life."[18] Men have superiority over women, and wives should be satisfied with this arrangement since it is God's will. In a statement that would make most contemporary women (and men) cringe, Calvin concludes, "Let the woman be content in her position of subjection, and not feel indignant because she has to play second fiddle to the superior sex."[19]

In considering 1 Cor. 14:34–36, Calvin concludes that since women are under subjection, they are also debarred from the authority to teach: "And there is no doubt that wherever natural propriety itself has had its effect, women in all ages have been excluded from the control of public affairs. And common sense tells us that the rule of women is improper and defective."[20] God has committed the office of teaching exclusively to men for a good reason (1 Tim. 2:12). Women cannot instruct others since that would give them authority over men, and this is not possible since they are subject to men.[21] Women, simply stated, are "born to obey," since the government of women is an "unnatural monstrosity."[22]

Although women in the Reformed tradition objected to such characterizations in the centuries that followed, their position in the church did not change much before the middle of the nineteenth century. As the research of Lois A. Boyd and R. Douglas Brackenridge indicates,

> Eighteenth-and nineteenth-century Presbyterian churchmen almost without exception held that women should be silent in the church, subordinate to male authority, submissive to doctrine and church order, and satisfied to function within their proper "sphere." . . . Women had virtually no acknowledged influence other than that exercised in the home, no status in that they

must remain silent in church councils, and no authority in that they were by definition subordinate to male decisions.[23]

The situation started to shift with the participation of women in the antislavery and women's suffrage movements and the lessons learned in the aftermath of the Civil War. In the latter part of the nineteenth century, women began to take a more active part in local and denominational mission organizations, serve as teachers and evangelists, and establish women's boards.[24] Their role in the church also began to change when more people began to study the Bible through the lens of modern critical exegesis—when it began to be seen that not all biblical texts should be given equal weight or the status of eternal divine decrees.

In the years that followed, Presbyterian women began to make a perceptible impact on the life of the Presbyterian Church. Their activities left a legacy that has continued: Donaldina Cameron rescued young Chinese girls from prostitution in San Francisco; Grace Hadley Dodge helped organize working girls' societies; Ashbel Green became the first president of the Women's Executive Committee of Home Missions (1878–1884); Sarah Smiley preached a temperance sermon in 1872 in Brooklyn; Narcissa Whitman became the first woman to cross the Rocky Mountains into Oregon; and Elizabeth Cady Stanton worked for women's rights, not only in reference to suffrage but in regard to their freedom to reinterpret the Bible.

By the close of the nineteenth century, women began to serve in churches in more visible ways. In 1889 Louisa Woolsey became the first Presbyterian woman to be ordained by a presbytery to the full work of the gospel ministry (Nolin Presbytery in the Cumberland Presbyterian Church), although it was not until 1921 that the church finally changed its constitution to include women as teaching elders.[25] During that period, several denominations began to ordain female deacons: the United Presbyterian Church of North America in 1906, the Cumberland Presbyterian Church in 1921, and the Presbyterian Church in the U.S.A. in 1923. The PCUSA changed its constitution to elect women as ruling elders in 1930. It was not until 1956, however, that the church voted to elect women as ministers of Word and Sacrament. In that year, the Rev. Margaret Towney was the first woman to be ordained as a pastor in the northern church; in 1965, the Rev. Rachel Hinderlite was the first to gain that office in the PCUS. Lois Stair was the first woman elected as the moderator of a UPCUSA General Assembly in 1972, and in 1978 Sarah B. Mosely assumed that office in the PCUS.[26]

The road to ordination, of course, was not as smooth as the description in a few sentences might indicate. Presbyterians debated the biblical and theological issues involved before and after the formal decisions were actually made.

In 1956, for example, the General Assembly of the PCUS approved an overture entitled "The Position of Women in the Church," which continued the dialogue begun as early as 1880.[27] The committee that wrote the report made a careful study of scriptural passages central to the debate, especially those in 1 Corinthians and 1 Timothy. They concluded that it was a mistake to take the admonitions recorded in those passages as "permanent" and "without exception" in order to bar women from ordained ministry in the church. Following the principle that the infallible rule of interpreting Scripture is found in Scripture itself, the report asserted that since there is ample evidence in the Bible that God endowed some women for ministry in the church (they cited Acts 2:17 specifically), and that Jesus and Paul actively included women in their ministries, that the manner of calling women into service is identical with the way men are called. Women should not be limited merely to educational positions over women and children, but should be elected as elders and deacons to serve the whole church. Paul's commands in 1 Cor. 14:34–35 and 1 Tim. 2:11–12, the report contended, should not be understood as permanently binding: "New ways of doing the same things are adopted to meet new conditions." The report concluded that a correct understanding of Paul's writings, of Jesus' teachings, and of the action of the Holy Spirit in the early church demonstrates how the Holy Spirit leads the people of God to changes in custom and policy.

Those of us who have served in the Presbyterian church since the middle 1960s can remember that even though women were officially accepted as equal partners in ministry more than a decade before, the way to full acceptance as ministers, church officers, and simply as individuals often remained difficult. Despite the fact that the Confession of 1967 prophetically called the church to "bring all men [*sic*] to receive and uphold one another as persons in all relationships of life: in employment, housing, education, leisure, marriage, family, church, and the exercise of political rights" (C-9.44), debates in the 1970s about the status of women continued on the floors of presbyteries, synods, and the General Assembly, as concerns were raised about the correct interpretation of Scripture. Women found it difficult to obtain ordination as ministers, and those who did were often surreptitiously blackballed from serving as senior pastors in large parishes. Some congregations actively worked to leave the Presbyterian church and join more conservative denominations because they disagreed so vehemently with those who favored the ordination of women. In 1974 much of the discussion in the church surfaced publicly in a judicial case decided by the General Assembly Judicial Commission of the UPCUSA. In this case, Walter Kenyon was eventually denied ordination as a pastor when he could not affirm the denomination's position that women were called to ministry with men.[28] A year later, more than twenty years after women were first ordained in the UPCUSA, Aurelia Fule wrote a pamphlet for the Council on Women and the Church entitled *A Biblical Inquiry: Should Women Keep Silence in the Churches?* It was still necessary to assert the need for the church to argue clearly against those who used the Bible to deny women ordination, and to maintain that "a clear position for the full partnership of women in the ministry . . . can and should be made."[29]

In the 1980s and 90s, concerns about the role of women in the church moved beyond issues of ordination. "Covenant and Creation: Theological Reflections on Contraception and Abortion" reflected the concern of the church in 1983 for a society in which "sexuality, conception, birth, and raising children" would be "issues of profound responsibility, fidelity, and care." In 1986 the 198th General Assembly approved a study called "Violations against the Image of God, Exploitation of Women," which explored sexual violence, exploitation in the workplace, and expressed concern about the ways prostitutes were treated in the United States.

In 1987 the next assembly approved a study entitled "Theology Written from Feminist Perspectives." The paper was written, as the introduction indicates, because feminism "represents spheres of concern which the church does not want to ignore." Major issues included stereotyping in the workplace and physical and verbal abuse in the family. The study attempted to show how feminist theologies reflect biblical truths and the validity of Reformed theology to women and men whose experiences call for new patterns of human relationships. The issue of abortion was taken up again in 1992 in "Do Justice, Love Mercy, Walk Humbly (Micah 6:8)" by the 204th General Assembly.[30]

A brief review of other concerns considered by various assemblies over a period years is a reminder of the difficult issues women have had to face in the recent past and must still confront in years to come: inclusive language (1975, 1985, 1994),[31] status of women in society (1967, 1972, 1975, 1983, 1985, 1986, 1988, 1991, 1999), feminization of poverty (1983, 1984), equal pay for jobs of comparable worth (1984), economic justice for women (1982, 1983, 1984, 1986), sexual misconduct (1991, 1993), reproductive rights (1995, 1998),[32] the increasing number of women leaving parish ministry (2000), the problems created by denominations that still deny women the right of ordination (2000), and the sexual abuse of children in religious institutions (2002).

Prospects: How Can the Text Be Rightly Used in the Future?

By the time Elizabeth Cady Stanton wrote *The Woman's Bible* in 1898, she had decided that the struggle for women's rights could not be won unless women also addressed issues of polity, theology, and biblical interpretation: "If the Bible teaches the equality of Woman, why does the church refuse to ordain women to preach the gospel, to fill the offices of deacons and elders, and to administer the Sacraments, or to admit them as delegates to the Synods, General Assemblies and Conferences of the different denominations?"[33] Although many leaders of the women's movement warned her to keep out of religious controversy, she was not dissuaded.[34] She was convinced that ministers (almost all male) and the church had become the primary obstacles to women's progress, and since she was proficient in Greek and Hebrew herself she was not about to be intimated by theological debate. As she indicated in a letter written to Sara Underwood in 1889, she was willing to take the debate all the way to the gates of heaven if need be. Imagining an encounter she might have with Paul face to face on the banks of the Jordan, Stanton indicated that as they walked arm in arm she would speak to him in a condescending manner to make certain that he was sure who was superior. She would wear no marks of subjugation like veils or bonnets, and she would challenge his writings directly, her Greek testament in hand, discussing his gross ideas on marriage. "Then if he airs any of those narrow theories he promulgated in Joppa, Ephesus and Damascus, we will have a discussion."[35]

(Note: One can only imagine how that discussion would go for Paul. The writer of this book hopes that Stanton and her successors will be more charitable to a white, male pastor who is presuming to come to conclusions about the future of women's ministry in the Presbyterian Church. Perhaps this section should be entitled a "Dialogue" or "Suggestions" in order to avoid similar difficult encounters in this world or the next.)

Despite the fact that women are now entering into most areas of employment in the United States—in ministry, medicine, education, dentistry, administration, politics, the armed forces, and construction—it is far from certain that they receive equal pay for equal work, regardless of what the law may say. Women still complain that rates of compensation and the distribution of perquisites are often a problem in the workplace. (The 212th General Assembly [2000] approved an overture that calls for gender equity regarding PC(USA) staff and their attendance of meetings of unofficial groups. The General Assembly voted that any employee can use church funds to attend events deemed relevant by her or his supervisor.)

One may still wonder if the church has fully accepted women as equal partners in ministry. Even if there is no statistical evidence to support an allegation, it is possible to contend that there is still considerable opposition in local churches to women clergy. The debate often takes place under the table and is seldom voiced in public, but anecdotal evidence indicates that some churches never really seriously consider women as candidates when vacancies occur. It can be hoped that such a condition is changing as more and more congregations are exposed to the ministries of women and have excellent experiences.

Other issues will also continue to concern women in the future. The work of the Advocacy Committee for Women's Concern (ACWC) in the last few years highlights some of the most obvious ones: sexual misconduct in the church, inclusive language, health care reform, affirmative action, violence at women's health clinics, child and international prostitution, child malnutrition, homelessness, and exploitation of women in the military.[36]

Presbyterians will also continue to be concerned about theological issues raised by feminist theologians. The controversy that surrounded the *Re-Imagining God, Church, Community* conference at the Global Theology Colloquium in November 1993 demonstrates how difficult it is for some church members to evaluate emerging theological positions. Many women are incorporating valuable feminist insights into biblical commentaries and are giving Christians an opportunity to examine theology and practice from fresh, new perspectives. But the strong reaction to the ideas and liturgy presented in Minneapolis demonstrates how critical continuing dialogue and education concerning women's issues are. Although many women left the conference stimulated and uplifted, others thought that heretical ideas had been espoused by referring to God's Wisdom in terms of the proper name Sophia. In response, the 206th General Assembly (1994) acknowledged how troubling the meeting had been for the church and recognized that a distinction needs to be drawn between theological dialogue, ecumenical/interfaith ritual, and the principles of Reformed worship. In the Assembly's opinion, some liturgical aspects at the meeting were open to question and debate. Nevertheless, the Assembly also reaffirmed its commitment to Jesus Christ as Lord and the validity of the principle that each new generation must be open to exploring and reexploring the purposes of God, as revealed in the Scriptures. The issue continues to create ripples in the church. In the summer of 2001, Mary Elva Smith, director of the Women's Ministries Program Area, asserted that she would like to have Presbyterians participate in another global women's conference that could restore the validity of feminist theology: "Feminist theology is with the Reformed tradition, which is not [set] in stone. . . . We're 'reformed yet always being reformed.' Feminist theology falls within the Reformed tradition. . . . It brings to it another perspective that needs to be heard."[37]

Other issues of international scope will also require the attention of women and men of faith in the future. Many women around the world do not have the legal rights that women have in the United States, and American Presbyterians will be called upon to support them with prayers, dollars, and presence overseas. Concerns about women's rights in Muslim countries in the Middle East, the problems faced by Arab women in Israel and the West Bank,[38] the continuing concern about the epidemic of AIDS throughout Africa, and issues raised by gender activists in South Africa[39] are only a few issues that can be mentioned.

One issue that is seldom discussed in the Presbyterian Church also needs to be faced. Although we have the closest of relationships with our Roman Catholic neighbors here and abroad and we are now pursuing high level conversations that may lead to further cooperation in the coming century, at some time the matter of women's rights in our sister denomination will have to be honestly faced. If Roman Catholics and members of other denominations continue to deny women partnership in ministry, and Presbyterians remain quiet or passive about the injustice involved, what can be said in favor of our witness or our profession to move beyond theological discussion to action? Will it be necessary to raise the issues in more direct and poignant ways in the future? Can we honestly contemplate the possibility of sitting around the same table someday soon when half of the members of some denominations are denied equality in ministry? These questions are not easy to ask, but theological integrity and the demands of the gospel may well bring us to that uncomfortable point sooner than we desire.

Perhaps some people think that it is better now, after so much progress has been made, for women and men of good intent to be silent for a time and not to continue to push so hard for women's rights throughout the world. But we have tried that approach before and we have seen that the rights of one group are closely related to those of another. It should be difficult to revel in our privileges when others have none. As Elizabeth Cady Stanton sagely laid it out,

> Let us remember that all reforms are interdependent, and that whatever is done to establish one principle on a solid basis, strengthens all. Reformers who are always compromising, have not yet grasped the idea that truth is the only safe ground to stand upon. The object of an individual life is not to carry one fragmentary measure in human progress, but to utter the highest truth clearly seen in all directions, and thus to round out and perfect a well balanced character.[40]

Questions for Study and Reflection

    1. In what capacities are women leading your congregation? When was the first woman ordained as an elder or deacon in your church's history? Has a woman ever served as a pastor in your congregation?

2. Look up some of the biblical passages concerning women mentioned in this chapter. What do you think Jesus' attitude toward women was? Look again at Gal. 3:28–29. How should this passage be understood in the life of your church or presbytery?

Chapter 7

You Have No Excuse When You Judge Others

Romans 2:1

Therefore you have no excuse, whoever you are, when you judge others; for in passing judgment on another you condemn yourself, because you, the judge, are doing the very same things.

Centrality of the Text

No issue in the last generation has created more controversy or been more vigorously debated by Presbyterians (and by Christians in other denominations) than the position of gays and lesbians within the church. Men and women of honest intentions, good conscience, and a sincere desire to base their opinions on their best understanding of biblical texts have taken opposite positions in a continuing disagreement that still threatens to fragment American denominations and undermine Christian unity at the beginning of the new century. The struggle for understanding cannot be sidestepped or ignored by anyone. Today every informed Christian is obligated to study the biblical and theological arguments and come to personal conclusions.

The Text

The first and second chapters of Romans, particularly Rom. 1:18–32 and 2:1–16, where Paul discusses pagan sinful behavior that distinguishes Jews from Greeks (i.e., non-Jews), are critically important among biblical texts because in them same-sex behavior clearly appears to be condemned: "For this reason God gave them up to degrading passions. Their women exchanged natural intercourse for unnatural, and in the same way also the men, giving up natural intercourse with women, were consumed with passion for one another. Men committed shameless acts with men and received in their own persons the due penalty for their error" (Rom 1:26–27). What can be said about this key passage? In this case, more plainly perhaps than in any other examined in this book, it is possible to see why one text cannot be considered in isolation if the opportunity for correct interpretation is to be achieved. Because Rom. 1–2 is part of a whole constellation of Old and New Testament verses that are analyzed when the question of the status of gays and lesbians is debated within the church, it is necessary to examine several other passages before taking Paul's critical testimony in Romans into account. As will be seen, some of them are not strictly relevant to the discussion, even though they are often used to criticize same-sex behavior.

Old Testament Texts[1]

Genesis 19:1–38

The first text that is usually considered is Gen. 19:1–38, the familiar account of Lot's strange encounter with two angels in the city of Sodom. After he invites them to come and stay overnight with him, mistaking them perhaps for ordinary travelers, the men of the city ("both young and old, all the people to the last man") surround the house and demand that Lot send out his guests so they can "know" them. The word "know," as the story of Adam and Eve indicates (Gen. 4:1), refers to sexual intercourse. Lot, indicating great hospitality and little sensitivity, offers them his two virgin daughters who are about to be married, but the sex-crazed denizens are not satisfied. According to the narrative, this tragic incident triggers the terrible destruction of Sodom and Gomorrah, places known thereafter for the violence and insatiable sexual appetite of their inhabitants.

Although references to the immorality and vileness of Sodom and Gomorrah appear in a number of places throughout the Old and New Testaments (see especially Ezek. 16:47–50; Matt. 10:15; 11:23–24; Luke 10:12; Rom. 9:29 [citing Isa. 1:9]; 2 Pet. 2:4–8; Jude 6–7), and despite the fact that the English word "sodomy" is derived from this story, most scholars agree that Gen. 19 does not deal specifically with a condemnation of homosexual behavior but with God's revulsion of sexual violence in all forms. What is more, the cities of Sodom and Gomorrah are also remembered in other biblical passages for their lack of social concern in general, not just for sexual crimes. Ezekiel 16:49–50 cites pride, excess of food, and prosperous ease that ignores the poor and needy. Second Peter 2:4–8 mentions ungodliness and depraved lust. Genesis 6:1–4 indicates that one of the sins that led to the great flood was the mating of the sons of God and human women; the account is followed in verse 5 with the comment "The LORD saw that the wickedness of humankind was great in the earth, and that every inclination of the thoughts of their hearts was only evil continually." It is likely that a similar condemnation of sexual contact between angels and humans is in mind in Gen. 19 as well.

Overall, it is necessary to conclude that the story of the attempted rape of the angels in Genesis is too bizarre and given too broad an interpretation in Scripture to be of specific help in determining whether gays and lesbians should be ordained. Any moral, caring, sensitive person, anywhere at any time, would be revulsed by the attitude displayed by the wild men of the city of Sodom.

Judges 19:1–30

A story that is even more unusual and difficult to understand, one that is also often examined in regard to the church's judgment of those engaging in same-sex relationships, is found in Judg. 19:1–30. Here a Levite from the hill country of Ephraim and his concubine stay at the home of a hospitable man in Jebus. During the night, the men of the city surround the house and demand that they be let in so they can have intercourse with their neighbor's guest. The man offers his virgin daughter and concubine, but they do not want them. When the traveler throws out his concubine, whom he loves, the men rape her repeatedly and leave her for dead. The guest cuts her up into twelve pieces, limb by limb, and sends the parts to all the tribes of Israel, and a war is started.

Again, there is nothing very helpful about this story for theological or ethical inquiry. Here and in Gen. 19, primary interest is in the ancient concept of the sanctity of hospitality, and there is much less concern about possible injustice to virgin daughters or the murder of concubines. The story has little to teach Christians who support equal sexual justice for all men and for women and affirm that sexual violence against any person is a violation of God's love command for the neighbor.

Leviticus 18:22 and 20:13

Other passages found in the Old Testament, particularly those in Leviticus, are more pertinent to our modern concern with sexuality, ordination, and the concept of Christian sexual ethics. In Lev. 18:22 a critical text reads, "You shall not lie with a male as with a woman; it is an abomination." Similarly, Lev. 20:13 says, "If a man lies with a male as with a woman, both of them have committed an abomination; they shall be put to death; their blood is upon them."

Leviticus is concerned primarily with the consecration of priests and proper conduct of the sacrificial worship of God. A distinctive mark of the congregation was the holiness of the Jews as compared to other people. Chapters 11–15 were written to maintain this holiness, culminating in chapter 16, where the Day of Atonement is described, a period that removed all uncleanness. The remaining chapters contain the Holiness Code (of which chapter 18 is a part), an extended sermon that tells the people how to avoid the punishment of God that leads to exile and destruction.

Although these texts are often cited in current discussions about sexuality and ordination, they are not as simple as they appear on the surface. Most scholars assert that the passages do not deal with homosexual behavior between individuals but are primarily concerned with temple prostitution and idolatrous actions that lead to the deification of sexual activities. Sacro-homosexual practices and female prostitution were established religious features in Canaan and in Mesopotamian, Egyptian, and Ugaritic cultures. Apparently some Jews used these sexual services when participating in Canaanite religions or tried to import them into Jewish temple practices, and the authors condemn them as acts that will destroy the purity and distinctiveness of God's people. More specific warnings are found in Deut. 23:17–18 and several passages in Kings (1 Kgs. 15:12; 22:46; 2 Kgs. 23:7), where the people are told that any Israelite who becomes a *qathesh* (male "temple prostitute," NRSV) or *qathesha* (female "temple prostitute") is "abhorrent to the LORD your God."

The Holiness Code in Leviticus 16 does not easily translate into contemporary Christian ethics. Sometimes interpreters have cavalierly rejected its commandments because parts of it are clearly irrelevant: prohibitions against sleeping with a woman during her menstrual period, concerns about sexual activities with farm animals, concerns about not eating blood, and so forth. Other parts of the code are generally still accepted by Christians today, however, and are honored: detailed prohibitions against adultery or incest in any form, revering one's father and mother, etc. Thus, it is clear that Leviticus provides a holiness code that requires historical understanding and examination. It cannot be adopted wholesale, because times and values have markedly changed since it was written; yet parts of it are as valuable to us as the Ten Commandments are. Because some of the texts are mainly concerned with activities in temple worship and are not directly relevant to twenty-first-century behavior, it will be necessary to turn to other biblical passages before proper judgment can be made about correct behavior for Christians today.

Stories of Ruth and Naomi, David and Jonathan

Before proceeding to the New Testament, it is useful to comment on two texts that are occasionally used to advocate gay and lesbian ordination and to contend that same-sex relationships are supported by biblical passages—the

well-known stories of the friendship between King David and his friend
Jonathan, and the connection between Naomi and Ruth. Even superficial
readings of the narratives involved indicate that such arguments run far
beyond the evidence. Ruth's decision to follow her mother-in-law shows her
faithfulness to God and has nothing to say about her sexuality. The fact that
the author of 1 Sam. 18:1–4 remarks that Jonathan loved David as his own
soul has no more to say about homosexuality than does Jesus' threefold question in John 21:15–23: "Peter . . . do you love me more than these?" None of
these passages remotely deal with critical questions regarding sexual behavior that concern the church today. The Bible recognizes several distinct types
of love, and we do a disservice to biblical narratives when we distort them by
reading our own concerns into them.

New Testament Texts

1 Corinthians 6:9

In 1 Cor. 6–8 Paul presents a list of ethical questions that particularly concerned Christians living in Corinth at the time the letter was written. No doubt
the same matters were important to thoughtful people living all through the
Roman Empire. Paul's discussion is remarkably similar to those found in the
writings of Seneca, Dio Chrystostom, and Philo Judaeus, where many of the
same questions are considered. In 1 Cor. 6:9–11, for example, he deals specifically with sexual activities that keep people out of the kingdom of God. The
first edition of the RSV indicates that sexual intercourse between men is meant
when it translates the Greek text, "Do not be deceived; neither the immoral,
nor idolaters, not adulterers, nor homosexuals, nor thieves, nor the greedy, nor
drunkards, nor revilers, nor robbers will inherit the kingdom of God." The
second edition changes "homosexuals" to "sexual perverts." Both editions
use one expression to translate two distinct Greek nouns, *malakoi* and
arsenokoitai that literally mean "soft, effeminate" and "men who sleep." Generally scholars understand them to refer to the passive and active partners in
homosexual relationships, both of whom are condemned by Paul.

Although many interpreters think that this is what the text does mean and
that Paul is critical in this text of homosexual behavior generally, along with
adultery, sexual promiscuity (fornication), and men having sex with female
prostitutes, recent research indicates that both editions of the RSV mistrans-
late the Greek. Thus the NRSV takes "sexual perverts" out of the second edition of the RSV and substitutes two expressions, "male prostitutes" and
"sodomites." Such an interpretation, for which there is considerable evidence
in Roman literature of the time, contends that what Paul condemns when he

uses the word *arsenokoitai* is not the homosexual type of activity that is practiced in the twenty-first century but one in which a man goes to a pagan temple and has sex with a male priest, under the delusion that he has thereby had contact with the god (a practice similar to that decried in Leviticus and Deuteronomy). Possibly Paul is also referring to a common practice in the ancient world called *pederasty*—which was often condemned by Roman writers as well—in which an adult man ("the man who sleeps") exploits a young boy (*malakos,* "soft, effeminate"). In these cases the boy was either an innocent victim who was being taken advantage of or was a "call boy" earning money by satisfying the "sodomite" who was his customer.

The proper interpretation of 1 Corinthians is further complicated by the fact that Paul is writing at a time when he expects the parousia to take place at any time. Because he thinks that the world will end momentarily, Paul also advises people against getting married (unless they are burning with sexual desire) and orders widows not to remarry, lest they be distracted with family matters when they should be focusing on preparing for the coming of the Lord.

A further point must be made about the relevance of this text to contemporary Presbyterian concern about the ordination of gays and lesbians. Christians generally agree that ordination in the church requires the highest moral conduct, and most believers no doubt find 1 Cor. 5–7 to be of invaluable help in the formulation of standards of ethical behavior. Yet it is possible to have difficulty with Paul's strong assertion that certain types of behavior will keep believers entirely out of God's kingdom, especially when we understand now that some of them (e.g., alcoholism) are primarily the result of addiction and illness and others can at times be classified as spiritual misdemeanors rather than felonies (greed, reveling, theft). The author of 1 Tim. 1:8–10 has a similar list of vices to be avoided by Christian people that also includes *arsenokoitai* (men sleeping with men; NRSV, "sodomites"). But he also includes other categories that are not strictly applicable to current questions about ordination, such as unholiness, profaneness (possibly to be translated "secularism" today), patricide and matricide, lying, gossiping, and the kidnapping of other people's slaves. The question we need to ask honestly and sincerely is, do we really understand the world to which Paul was writing and is it enough like ours to draw generalizations about ordination of officers? As Victor Paul Furnish points out, human sexuality is an infinitely more complex phenomenon than Paul and his contemporaries could have imagined:

It would be unfair to charge Paul with näiveté or ignorance in the matter of homosexuality. Such evidence as we have suggests he was as informed as anyone could have been in his day. Indeed, *we* would be the naïve ones were we to ignore the data available to us in our own day, supposing that Paul's teaching alone is sufficient to answer our questions about right and wrong in this difficult matter.[2]

Romans 1:24–32

Having considered other biblical texts, we can now return to Romans, where Paul discusses the ways in which Gentiles, people who are not Jews and not yet Christians either, keep themselves out of the kingdom. Listing vices that call down the wrath of God and cause God to give people over to the consequences of their own sinfulness, he says that the anger of God falls on ungodliness and wickedness of those who suppress the truth. Ignoring things that are clearly divinely prohibited and are unnatural, these people go ahead and do things that God does not want them to do, surrendering to lusts of passion, worshiping idols, women having intercourse with women (this is the only mention of lesbianism in the Bible), men having intercourse with men, murder, strife, deceit, craftiness, boastfulness, foolishness, cold-heartedness, and gossip. They have no excuse, Paul writes, and since they do not see fit to believe in God, God gives them over to a debased mind and immoral lifestyle.

The argument that is often made on the basis of this text is that these activities, like those mentioned in 1 Cor. 6 and 1 Tim. 1, constitute such sinfulness and breaches of fundamental Christian ethics that people who willingly practice them have, by their own actions and their own refusal to obey God's natural laws, put themselves outside of God's favor and therefore cannot be ordained as officers in the church. If they repent, if they turn back to God, however, then all things can be forgiven, even lesbianism, homosexuality, and murder, and they can be considered for church office.

But what about the context of Paul's overall argument in Romans? In Romans 1 Paul says that the Gentiles have sinned and are far below God's standards. In chapter 2 he tells the Jews that they have no excuse either because with their emphasis on a puritanical keeping of the law they have also missed the point of God's love. In 3:21–23, he concludes that *all* have sinned and fallen short of the glory of God. Another way of interpreting this text, then, is to see that when it comes to being ordained Christians, we are all sinners and so no matter who your elder, deacon, or pastor is, you have to pick your sinner! There is no other kind of church officer to have. To single out those out who have sexual relations with people of the same sex, based on Paul's argument, misses the point. It is not just gays or lesbians who may be involved in unwholesome relationships. It is true of people who are married, of those who live together in an unmarried state, of those who associate with other human beings in nonsexual activities. It is true of all believers whether we keep the Ten Commandments with fanatical fastidiousness or are as free as Paul later considered himself to be (Gal. 5:1). There are no exceptions, there are no excuses, there are no acceptable rationalizations. We have *all* fallen short, and none of us is worthy of God's grace or the call to serve the church in the name of the Son of God.

Use in the Reformed Tradition and the Presbyterian Church

Since Presbyterians have been debating issues around the ordination of gays and lesbians as church officers at length during four different decades and because the church's position is well known, it is unnecessary to do more than provide a brief review of General Assembly actions here.

The controversy began among Presbyterians, contrary to what is often assumed, not in 1978 when the General Assembly took definitive action, but some five years earlier with the publication of an issue of a magazine published by the Program Agency of the United Presbyterian Church U.S.A. called *Trends*. In the July-August 1973 issue entitled "Homosexuality: Neither Sin nor Sickness," articles by eight different authors urged the church to consider a new perspective on homosexuality, a position that surprised and shocked many church members. As the editors wrote in an introductory article, "Is homosexuality a manifestation of sin? Is it a sickness? No, on both counts, say the authors in this issue. In so doing, they depart markedly from the traditional responses to these questions. Radical thinking? Perhaps so. Nonetheless, we have chosen to emphasize this perspective because we believe it is most in keeping with the Biblical doctrine of grace for all persons." For many readers, the positions that not all Scripture passages have the same authority, that homosexual acts might fall in the same categories of personal choice as cutting or not cutting your hair, and that the church has to deal with its own oppression of homosexuals awakened angry thoughts of denial in most Presbyterians, and in a few, a vision of forgotten Christian freedom.[3]

Responding to concerns about the questions raised in *Trends* and other publications, the UPCUSA General Assembly issued a statement that declared that Presbyterians could only continue in the Reformed tradition by approaching the subject of homosexuality with "love, compassion, prayer, and honesty."[4] Knowing that it is always possible for "more light" to break forth from the Bible through the action of the Holy Spirit, the 188th Assembly (1976) nevertheless reaffirmed that the practice of homosexuality is sin. At the same time, it directed that a task force be established to study Christian approaches to homosexuality and the ordination of avowed practicing homosexuals. In 1978 the 190th Assembly rejected the report of that task force, which called for a radically new view of homosexuality. Concluding that homosexuality is not God's wish for humanity, the church established what was later called "definitive guidance," a directive which said that avowed, practicing homosexuals could not be ordained as pastors, elders, or deacons. In 1979 the PCUS Assembly took a similar position.

In 1985, after years of continuing controversy at nearly every subsequent meeting of the General Assembly, the Permanent Judicial Commission ruled that "definitive guidance" was the law of the church, and that individual presbyteries and churches could not obey it or disobey it at will. Although another task force in 1991 reexamined biblical passages traditionally used to support the church's position and found them to be misinterpreted, irrelevant, or misunderstood, their recommendations were not adopted.

During the next year, the attempted installation of a self-affirming lesbian as copastor at the Downtown Presbyterian Church in Rochester, New York, attracted national attention. In spite of the fact that the Rev. Jane Adams Spahr's installation was approved by the Presbytery of Genesee Valley and the Synod of the Northeast, the Permanent Judicial Commission of the General Assembly rejected their arguments in a ruling in November 1992, and the congregation (along with other organizations) hired her as an evangelist rather than a pastor.

In 1993 when several presbyteries adopted overtures calling for the overturning of "definitive guidance," the Assembly again reaffirmed the current constitutional law that self-affirming, practicing homosexuals could not be ordained. At the same time, it ordered a three-year study of the central issues throughout the whole church. At the end of the period of dialogue, which was a time of painful debate and division in many congregations and presbyteries, the 208th General Assembly (1996) voted to change the constitution so that it clearly and explicitly stated the church's position. The so-called Amendment B, the fidelity and chastity amendment (now G-6.0106b), states,

> Those who are called to office in the church are to lead a life in obedience to Scripture and in conformity to the historic confessional standards of the church. Among those standards is the requirement to live either in fidelity within the covenant of marriage between a man and a woman (W-4.9001), or chastity in singleness. Persons refusing to repent of any self-acknowledged practice which the confessions call sin shall not be ordained and/or installed as deacons, elders, or ministers of the Word and Sacrament.

An attempt to change those standards (proposed Amendment A) and take out the reference to homosexual practices was rejected by the Assembly in 1998.[5] Despite the fact that several overtures were presented again by presbyteries wishing to delete G-6.0106b from the *Book of Order,* the 211th Assembly (1999) rejected them and voted to recommend that the church take a two-year moratorium on votes on issues concerning homosexuality. In 2000, by a vote of 268-251, the Assembly sent a proposed amendment to the presbyteries for their vote that called for the banning of church officials from participating in services that pronounced blessings or approvals of same-sex unions. The amendment did not receive the requisite number of presbyteries voting in the affirmative, and it failed in the spring of 2001.

Later in that same year, however, the 213th General Assembly approved an overture that was a surprising departure from the actions of previous assemblies. By a vote of 317-208, a proposed constitutional amendment was sent to the presbyteries to take an entirely new tack and strike G-6.0106b altogether. By the same action, it was recommended to provide an addition to G-6.0106a that would leave the question of the ordination of gays and lesbians entirely up to presbyteries and local sessions: "Suitability to hold office is determined by the governing body where the examination for ordination or installation takes place, guided by scriptural and constitutional standards, under the authority and Lordship of Jesus Christ." The Assembly also voted to recommend the repeal of the "authoritative interpretation" approved in 1978 and reaffirmed in 1993 ("definitive guidance"), and declare it of "no further force or effect." These proposed changes were overwhelmingly rejected by a large majority of presbyteries in the next few months in 2001 and 2002, and G-6.0106b remains in force.

Prospects: How Can the Text Be Rightly Used in the Future?

Considering the ways in which Presbyterians have responded to the biblical perspectives over the past few years, and the continuing pattern of debate, argument, and dialogue that surrounds an issue so important to the church, Presbyterians may wonder how the church can ever resolve the sharp disagreements that still exist about same-sex relationships and questions of ordination. Although it is not possible to predict how the presbyteries will vote in subsequent years, it is probably naive to assume that one vote will bring the matter to a close. The frequency of public debate may be limited by the advent of biennial assemblies (as approved by the 214th General Assembly), but the decisions of upcoming General Assemblies will probably still be determined by the consciences of the particular commissioners attending them, and what will happen in the years to come is impossible to say.

Perhaps it will be helpful for all Presbyterians to think one more time about the biblical witness and to consider the fundamental scriptural principles that must be applied before a final decision about such a divisive matter is attempted again. The solution will no doubt involve a new way of thinking for some members and movement beyond the few biblical texts that are normally considered. If, in the first half of the nineteenth century, the church had merely confined its witness to basic texts that only spoke about slavery, it might never have moved to embrace human rights in the name of the love of God and the grace of Jesus Christ prior to the beginning of the Civil War. If, as the Confession of 1967 asserts, the Scriptures provide the "witness without parallel" to our faith and action, at least two questions need to be considered. Are there any standards of judgment that were used in the past that are no longer applicable? Are there other scriptural passages that should be examined to help us out of the impasse?

In regard to the first question, it needs to be acknowledged that one biblical principle Presbyterians will have to jettison is that all biblical passages must be accorded equal interpretative weight in a given discussion or debate. A view of Scripture that maintains an "all or nothing" principle leads to a domino hermeneutical effect, that is, if one passage is set aside, all other passages fall with it. But, in fact, that is not the way most Christians understand the Bible. Although such a view may be simpler and may require less thinking on the part of interpreters, it is not logical, and it is not the way Bible texts themselves teach us to think. In Matt. 4:1–11, and the parallels in the other Synoptic Gospels, for example, Satan challenges Jesus to adopt a style of ministry that is based on several faulty interpretations of Old Testament passages. But Jesus does not succumb to the notion that because God has miraculous power to make bread from stone, that he has the right to ask for food for himself (or the hungry masses) while he is being tempted in the wilderness. Instead, he counters with text from Deut. 8:3 that is more to the point: "One does not live by bread alone, but by every word that comes from the mouth of the Lord." On two more occasions, the tempter tries to lure Jesus from his calling by quoting Old Testament texts, but each time his arguments are refuted: "Worship the Lord your God, and serve only" God.[6]

What are we doing when we choose one Old Testament text rather than another? What happens when a New Testament passage is judged to be more appropriate as God's word today than another? Are we guilty of relativism? Are we playing one text off against another? Do we lack standards altogether? Actually, when we choose one text over another, our action is positive rather than negative because we are exercising our responsibility as mature Christians to understand Scripture in context and allow the Holy Spirit to enable us to interpret it as it applies to us in our own situation rather than someone else's. If, for example, as Leslie Weatherhead used to point out, we see a clear conflict between the teachings of Jesus and something taught in the Old Testament, we should not have any trouble deciding between the two.[7] It should not be difficult for us to reject teachings that call for the total destruction of the enemy when Jesus teaches us to love the enemy. It should not be a hardship to refuse to kill witches even when the Old Testament commands it if we have an understanding of the terrible atrocities committed by Christians in the past when they thought they were obeying God's word in a literal sense.

In regard to our ongoing debate about the ordination of gays and lesbians, it needs to be recognized that there are biblical texts that are of equal, or perhaps even greater value, than the ones that are traditionally consulted on this issue, and that they should also be taken into consideration when we make constitutional decisions. In Mark 9:38–39, for example, John comes to Jesus and says that he saw someone casting out demons in Jesus' name but that he stopped him because he was not properly enrolled as a disciple. Jesus tells him not to exclude people like that from ministry because whoever performs a deed of power in his name will not be able soon afterward to speak evil of him. And he adds, "Whoever is not against us is for us."

When we turn to the parallel passages in Matthew, however, a very different attitude prevails. Matthew's Jesus' says just the opposite (Matt. 12:30): "Whoever is not with me is against me." The reason for the stark contrast is not difficult to discover. As one commentator puts it, "The Markan community is 'world open,' while the Matthean community appears as 'world concerned' and suspicious of those outside the community."[8] To put it in nonsociological terms, it could be said that the difference between the two texts has to do with boundaries and walls. Mark is writing for a Gentile congregation and is trying to open the doors of the church and welcome people in. Matthew, however, believes that good fences make good neighbors. Since he is battling elite Jewish leaders and those in power in Rome for the minds of a church in the midst of terrible struggle after the fall of Jerusalem in A.D. 70, he wants to draw the wagons around in a circle to protect those who believe. As L. Michael White says, "In times of crisis, when the group feels that its identity or existence is threatened, it will tend to cause key defining boundaries to be hardened and symbolic markers to receive more stress."[9]

In a seminal study entitled *The First Urban Christians*, Wayne Meeks analyzes what happens in the church when it adopts a crisis mentality. Speaking of Paul's teaching in 1 Cor. 10 about eating meat offered to idols, Meeks comments on Paul's flexibility and his willingness to eat or not to eat, depending on his companions at supper. Paul does not adopt such an open spirit because he wants to pit one Scripture passage against another, because he is a pluralist, or because he has no firm beliefs himself. Rather, he indicates that he does so because he knows that those who have strong faith have weak boundaries and that those who have weak faith need strong boundaries. If you have a strong faith, boundaries are not that important because by letting people in who differ from you, you have nothing to lose and everything to gain. But if your faith is weak, you must remain rigid and against those outside your in-group because you are afraid that you might lose the little you already have.[10]

Clearly, it is not fair to apply such an analysis to everyone who opposes the ordination of gays and lesbians. People of open, loving faith can and do differ on the meaning of extending the welcoming love of Jesus to others. Nevertheless, there is a sense in which the current debate seems to be solidifying around the question of boundaries and walls. Robert Frost certainly has it correct when he reminds us of the danger of loving a wall. In his poem "Mending Wall," a neighbor insists on mending the rock wall that defines mutual property lines. This leads the poet to wonder about motive:

> "Before I built a wall I'd ask to know
> What I was walling in or walling out."[11]

What kind of faith do we want to project to others in the years to come? For many Presbyterians the debate is framed much more differently than it was in 1978. It is no longer a question of circling wagons or repairing ethical moats but deciding what right we have to exclude others from Christ's church on the basis of our interpretation of a few questionable Bible texts.

In Mark 10:2–12, to give another example, Jesus speaks out against divorce. Those who remarry, he clearly says, are guilty of a breach of the Ten Commandments. They have committed the sin of adultery. Although it is difficult to think that Jesus would close the door in the face of so many people who have been through the pain of separation and divorce, that is what the text says, and there is no easy way around it without some fancy hermeneutical legerdemain. Strictly speaking, then, all of us who have been divorced, regardless of the circumstances, are guilty of breaking the commandments and should surrender ordination rights. Prior to 1973, when the constitution of the United Presbyterian Church was changed, pastors and officers were deemed guilty of adultery if they remarried after divorce. For years that is what the church believed, and during those years many faithful Christian leaders suffered fear and unimaginable pain because their church determined that they had committed sinful acts which excluded them from ministry in the future. Yet that is not what Presbyterians believe any more because believers realize that although Jesus remains our Lord, our interpretation of his words do not remain static. We understand that people find themselves in the midst of divorce for many different reasons and that it is contrary to the gospel to exclude them from the church's work on that basis alone. When we think of Jesus encountering those who have been through painful separation and divorce, we simply do not believe that he faces them as judge, but as healer and friend.

Or consider John 9. In this passage Jesus heals a man born blind. The Pharisees ask Jesus who sinned, the man or his parents? Jesus tells them that sin has nothing to do with it, but that the man's healing will be used to show God's glory. The Pharisees, reacting to selected passages in the Old Testament, choose to accuse a man who is a victim of a terrible handicap of being a sinner. In Lev. 21:16–21 it is said that no one who is handicapped in any way may be a priest or offer sacrifice to God. No one who has a "blemish" may apply, no one who is blind or lame or has a mutilated face or a limb too long, no one who has a broken foot or hand. In the Dead Sea Scrolls, furthermore, it was decreed that blind men were not allowed to fight in the final battle between good and evil (IQM 7, 4ff.). Somehow these interpreters had ignored other texts in the Holiness Code that ordered Israel to give special consideration to the blind and deaf (Lev. 19:14). They did not consider Scripture passages that saw their healing as a sure sign of the in-breaking of the kingdom (Isa. 35:5–6). They ignored Isa. 42 and other texts in which the Messiah is compared to God's blind servant. Jesus, however, refuses to accept their line of thinking and demonstrates how those who are marginalized and the most despised by society are often those whom God chooses to reflect divine glory and illustrate the meaning of true compassion.

One more text that is helpful is the description of the Jerusalem Conference recounted in Acts 15. At that meeting, the major discussion revolved around the admission of uncircumcised people into the church. Some of the brothers (presumably some of the sisters too) argued that "unless you are circumcised according to the custom of Moses, you cannot be saved." Luke says in the narration that there was "no small dissension and debate," as translated with characteristic understatement in the NRSV. The Greek text clearly indicates, however, that they were so angry with each other (the words are literally used to describe civil strife or sedition) that they were almost on the verge of a riotous situation and serious division. Somehow the disagreeing Christians were able to continue their discussion and work out an agreement that allowed those who did not meet Old Testament standards to find their proper place at Christ's table. What had once seemed to be repugnant and contrary to God's will was understood in a new way, and the believers were able to respond to a new word of the Lord and head in a new direction.

Certainly in the Presbyterian Church the issue that stands before us will not go away. It may not be resolved in a short period of time. The lessons from history in the debates in our denomination about evolution and abolition of slavery do not offer great hope to those who pray for quick solutions. Unfortunately, while Christians continue their debates about the ordination of gays and lesbians, faithful Christians are being hurt by our bias. They are suffering injustice and prejudice and we need to wonder how long God will tolerate unloving treatment of more of Jesus' brothers and sisters. The studies in this chapter demonstrate, moreover, that there is ample evidence to suggest, even on the basis of a Reformed understanding of Scripture, that the current stance of the denomination is restrictive and could be considered to be contrary to the loving teaching of our Lord, as well as out of keeping with our own principles for interpreting the Bible (see especially the statements of various General Assemblies reviewed in the introduction). All of us need to be in prayer, not only for those who disagree with us but for those who are being hurt by the church's refusal to allow neighbors a rightful place in the church's leadership.

Above all, it may be that the church needs to consider, with absolute seriousness, who it is that is being walled in or out by our insistence that gays and lesbians are not worthy of ordination. If Matt. 28 provides a worthwhile guideline, we may eventually find out that we are walling out Christ himself, for if we cannot see Christ in our neighbor (whether that neighbor is a friend or enemy), we will not be able to see the Lord at all.

In many communities today, people who might be interested in taking part in Presbyterian church life are having serious second thoughts. If the Presbyterian Church teaches that gays and lesbians are not welcome as officers, those who do not understand the fine points of church polity can be forgiven if they assume that what we really mean is that gays and lesbians are not welcome at all. How is it possible, they wonder, when gays and lesbians—their friends, neighbors, and family members—serve with honesty and competence as doctors, lawyers, teachers, mayors, leaders of the chamber of commerce, and members of Congress, that these same people can be perceived by Presbyterians to be incompetent and morally unsuitable to serve God? If we say that the exclusion of certain people is something we learned from Christ, then how can non-Presbyterians avoid one of two conclusions—either that it is Christ himself who shuts the door on their friends and neighbors, or that we simply do not know Christ well enough to say anything in his name? Although we do not base our theology or our polity on public perception, it may be that we should listen to those around us. Do we want to be a church known for its openness and love, or one that stands in the mind of the community as the fellowship of the closed door?

Frequently Presbyterians worry that if those engaged in same-sex relationships are allowed to lead the church, we will be guilty of abandoning the high standards we require of church officers and pastors. Certainly the question is worthy of careful consideration. It will not be easy to rethink our theology of Christian sexual ethics. How will we determine the limits for pastors, elders, and deacons? There is no reason to think that we will cease to believe that those who are sexually promiscuous, who make sex their idol, who corrupt children or young people, who take advantage of other adults are not the kind of people we want in ministry. But a bigger question also needs to be faced. How can we stand before our Lord and Savior and say that gays and lesbians who are faithful to one another must be excluded from leadership in the church when all they themselves may want in their relationships is personal encounter, love, and fairness? What is the primary purpose of same-sex relationships, after all? Is it for a good purpose? Is it to be close to other people? Is it finally for love? Then wherein is its tragic fault?

Perhaps when it comes to questions of ordination, the time has come when Presbyterians must jettison medieval and Victorian concepts that decree that sexuality is the chief criterion that decides whether or not individuals enter the kingdom of God. Sexuality is important and says a lot about who we are as human beings, but when it comes to loving others, most of us still have a lot to learn. Perhaps it is time for all Christians to listen more carefully to the Lord, and before we build a wall, be sure that we know whom we are walling in or walling out.

Questions for Discussion and Reflection

1. Has your session taken a position on the question of ordaining gays and lesbians as church officers? Do you agree with it? How does it compare to the stance generally taken by your presbytery or the one currently found in the *Book of Order*?
2. What Scripture passages, in your opinion, are the most important in regard to this question? Can you see why some texts are not as important as some people think they are?
3. What do you think will happen to our denomination if it continues to be so divided over this issue? What should happen?

Chapter 8

He Is Our Peace
Ephesians 2:14

For he is our peace; in his flesh he has made both groups into one and has broken down the dividing wall, that is, the hostility between us.

Centrality of the Text

*T*he final chapter brings the discussion full circle in the search to understand biblical texts that make us Presbyterians. The conclusion is the beginning, since Jesus Christ is advent and ending, alpha and omega. If faith begins with the commitment to Jesus as Lord, it finds maturation when it is realized that—in a world in which believers are tormented by stress, turmoil, and doubt, and in a time when the nations are still pulled apart by continuing violence, and even terrorist attacks on major U.S. cities—peace can only be found in him, since Jesus is our peace. Perhaps at no time since nuclear annihilation was a daily threat has there been a greater need to understand this central Christian belief.

The Text

The primary text is Eph. 2:14, where the author of Ephesians asserts that Jesus can remove all barriers, even those that have been causing conflict between Jews and Gentiles.

It may surprise us to read that Jesus *is* our peace when we are more accustomed to thinking that he is the one who *makes* peace or *proclaims* it (Eph. 2:15, 17). Yet the author is applying broader, more universal terms and wants to assure Christians that Jesus has the power to bring all people together, no matter how far apart they may appear to be. The connection is similar to the cosmic origin claimed for Jesus in John 1:1–14 where it is said that Jesus does more than preach the word; he *is* the Word from the beginning.[1]

The confession that Jesus is our peace reminds us of another important truth as well. In our attempt to bring about reconciliation and peace in our families, communities, nation, and around the world, we are often forced to recognize that we cannot do it by ourselves. As limited human beings, we do not have the power. As sinners, we often do not have the will or the wisdom. As Christians, we know that we need Jesus if real peace is to occur. We simply cannot do it without him.

The text that appears in 2:14–15 is probably a hymn that had been used in services of worship by the early church. Perhaps it was well known to the readers and called forth an immediate positive response, much as "Amazing Grace" or "Holy, Holy, Holy" would with us. Hymns have been used before in Ephesians to remind readers of the fundamental elements of their faith (1:22–23; 2:4–7; see also Col. 1:21–22).[2]

The writer indicates that the division and hatred that has existed between Jews and Christians for years has now been broken down because of the presence of Jesus Christ. This peace, as verse 13 demonstrates, is brought about by his sacrificial death. As Paul says in Gal. 3:28, all distinctions are dissolved in him since all who believe in Christ put on Christ, are in him, become like him, and act through him.

The metaphor of the wall provides a graphic illustration of how mistrust and suspicion destroys relationships. In Greek it refers to a fence, railing, or hedge used for separation or protection (Isa. 5:5; Matt. 21:33). In Ephesians it may describe several different realities. Possibly the dividing wall that separated the Court of the Gentiles from the rest of the Jerusalem Temple is in mind. Gentiles who passed beyond it were subject to the penalty of death. Since the letter was written after the destruction of the Temple by the Romans in A.D. 70, it is obvious that such a wall no longer existed, and the remaining ruins of the Temple might indicate to Christians that God wants to obliterate the division between Jews and Christians and that in Jesus they can be made one. It is also possible that the wall mentioned in Ephesians is a symbol for the Jewish law and the way in which it was interpreted (2:15). Since rabbis later described the law as a "fence" erected by God to keep out Gentile contamination, Eph. 2:14 may point to the fact that the demands of the law are now fulfilled in Christ. A third alternative is that the wall mentioned here symbolizes the sinfulness of all believers that separates them from God (Isa. 59:2; Rom. 1:24, 26). In Jesus' death and resurrection they are reconciled to God, and the hostility that once characterized their relationship has come to an end.

It is likely, of course, that all three meanings are in mind, since for the author, Jesus has the power to terminate all conflict. It is part of fundamental Christian confidence that he still has the authority to tear down all the barriers that exist in the church and the world. It is a basic element of our faith that we trust Jesus in all aspects of life, even those that are the most hostile and frightening.

In Rom. 5:1, for example, Paul connects our ability to bring about peace with the nature of our relationship to God, bringing us again to the centrality of the concept of justification by faith: "Therefore, since we are justified by faith, we have peace with God through our Lord Jesus Christ." That peacemaking and righteousness go together was an insight of the writers of the Old Covenant in their expectation of the Messiah's coming. When love and faithfulness meet, the psalmist writes, righteousness and peace will kiss each other (Ps. 85:10); when the Lord reigns, "the effect of righteousness will be peace, and the result of righteousness, quietness and trust forever" (Isa. 32:17; see Isa. 52:7; Ezek. 34:25; 37:26; Nah. 1:15).

Practically speaking, of course, we know that writing about peace does not necessarily create it. The prophets were aware that some people who declare peace are falsely optimistic while others are deliberately being deceptive in order to exploit those who are in desperate situations (Jer. 6:14; 8:11; 14:19; Ezek. 7:25; 13:10), preaching peace when there is no peace.

A proper antidote against false prescriptions is found in the Sermon on the Mount, where Jesus teaches that the peacemakers are blessed or happy (Matt. 5:9). Peacemaking can only come from an inner attitude, a commitment of the heart based on a relationship with Jesus Christ that is nurtured through prayer and frequent meditation upon the Scriptures. It results in a spiritual maturity achieved by continually being in the presence of the living God.

Jesus' language indicates, of course, that peacemaking is more than inner calm; it also involves active participation in the real world. It is peace*making,* not just peace *talking,* or peace *thinking,* peace *wishing,* or even peace *praying.* The Greek literally refers to those who are peace *doers* (*eirēnopoioi*). Peacemaking demands real work, active effort, and engagement in a creative process to make things happen.

Peacemaking is more than wishful thinking. It is the most difficult human interaction imaginable because Jesus indicates that it requires us to do things we are not inclined by nature to do—to turn the other cheek and love the enemy who hates us and wants us dead (Matt. 5:38–48). Peacemaking clearly is a part of the central message of the Christian faith. It is reflected in the light of Christmas, the joy of the presence of the Messiah (Luke 1:79; 2:14); it is the eschatological hope that some day there will be war no more (Isa. 9:7); it speaks of the final hope for all God's children around a single table (Rev.

3:20). Peacemaking is the vocation of every Christian. It is a goal we are commanded to pursue. It is our daily work in the home, the church, the community, and the world (Rom. 12:18; 14:19; Gal. 6:10; 1 Pet. 3:11).

Use in the Reformed Tradition and the Presbyterian Church

Presbyterians have made peacemaking a major component of faith and action since the early 1960s and have written a great deal about its place in the Reformed tradition.[3] Basic attitudes toward government and the freedom with which Presbyterians embrace peacemaking have been strongly influenced by John Calvin, particularly his comments in book 4, chapter 20 of the *Institutes*. As John T. McNeill points out, although Calvin was respectful of the power of the kings, he was far from subservient to them.[4] Rather than merely considering himself a subject, he assumed the role of a counselor to rulers. In Calvin's opinion, although God called those in power to their positions, they had to carry out their duties for the good of their subjects. Theirs is a holy vocation, one that calls them to pursue clemency, moderation, and justice. Although Calvin generally thought that citizens should obey all rulers, even tyrannical ones (in keeping with his understanding of Rom. 13), he also insisted on the ultimate right to resistance, since he considered it to be the duty of believers to oppose violence and cruelty (*Institutes* 4.20.31). Although it was his preference that believers should be willing to suffer before they opposed their government, their ultimate choice should never be to obey human rulers instead of the living God. The Lord alone is the King of Kings, and if a king or government decrees anything against God's commands, he urges them to "let it go unesteemed" (4.20.32).

Somewhat similarly, the Westminster Confession (1648) declares that God has ordained magistrates to be obedient when they rule over the people, for God's glory and for the public good (C-6.127–30). It is lawful for Christians to accept and execute the office of magistrate "to maintain piety, justice, and peace, according to the wholesome laws of each commonwealth," even waging war if necessary (6.128). Westminster carefully draws distinctions between the rights of church and state, however, proclaiming that magistrates cannot assume the administration of the Word and sacraments; they must not interfere in matters of faith but must protect the church and allow all ecclesiastical persons to enjoy "the full, free, and unquestioned liberty of discharging every part of their sacred functions, without violence or danger" (C-6.129). Although it is the duty of the people to pray for magistrates and to honor their decisions even if they demonstrate infidelity or difference in religion, it is also made clear in the section on Christian liberty that God alone is the Lord of conscience and has left believers free from human doctrines and commands that are in any way contrary to the word of God, or "beside it in matters of faith or worship" (C-6.109). "So that to believe such doctrines, or to obey such commandments out of conscience, is to betray true liberty of conscience; and the requiring an implicit faith, and an absolute and blind obedience, is to destroy liberty of conscience, and reason also" (C-6.109).

The Reformed concept of politics has led Presbyterians to vigorous and active involvement in all levels of American life, usually in the attempt to improve government through peaceful means, but at some critical times in our history, through the drive for radical change. Participation in the Revolutionary War, the fight for the abolition of slavery, the struggle to overthrow Hitler during World War II, the resistance to the Vietnam War, and actions to reduce the proliferation of nuclear weapons from 1954 to the present clearly demonstrate the frequent resolve of "Presbyterians individually and collectively to lobby, petition, pray or otherwise try to influence the governments of the USA and other nations of the world."[5]

The controversy over the Vietnam War was particularly divisive, and Presbyterians strongly disagreed about U.S. involvement in the fighting in Asia. The Confession of 1967 expressed the growing consensus that participation in the war was wrong:

> God's reconciliation in Jesus Christ is the ground of the peace, justice, and freedom among nations which all powers of government are called to serve and defend. The church, in its own life, is called to practice the forgiveness of enemies and to commend to the nations as practical politics the search for cooperation and peace. This search requires that the nations pursue fresh and responsible relations across every line of conflict, even at risk to national security. (C-9.45)

In 1969 the UPCUSA General Assembly supported the right of believers to object to a particular conflict on pacifist grounds, and called for amnesty for draft resisters and deserters. In 1976 the PCUS called upon President Ford to grant a full pardon to all who refused to serve in the war. In that same year, both Assemblies objected to the waging of war merely for the purpose of sustaining a high standard of living.

Because of the controversy over Vietnam in 1975 and the growing danger of nuclear holocaust, the 187th General Assembly (UPCUSA) commissioned the Advisory Council on Church and Society to reassess the concept of peacemaking and the direction of U.S. foreign policy in the light of biblical and confessional faith. A special task force was appointed, and its seminal report, "Peacemaking: The Believers' Calling," was approved in 1980. Adopted by the PCUS General Assembly in 1981, and reaffirmed by the reunited church in 1983, it still provides fundamental guidelines for Presbyterian peacemaking activities in the twenty-first century.

In words that have a profoundly contemporary ring, considering the violence that racks the nations in the opening years of this new century, "Peacemaking: The Believers' Calling" urges Christians to respond in faith, rather than trust in arms:

> Ominous clouds hang over human history. There are frightening risks in the continuing arms race and looming conflicts over diminishing energy resources as centers of power struggle for control. . . . But we believe that these times, so full of peril and tragedy for the human family, present a special call for obedience to our Lord, the Prince of Peace. The Spirit is calling us to life out of death.[6]

The report urges Presbyterians to develop a new sense of "the oneness of the world" and to strive anew for economic and political justice in the whole human family. The Assemblies declared peacemaking to be the responsibility of all believers and endorsed three major guidelines:

- The church is faithful to Christ when it is engaged in peacemaking.
- The church is obedient to Christ when it nurtures and equips God's people as peacemakers.
- The church bears witness to Christ when it nourishes the moral life of the nation for the sake of peace in the world.

The report concluded with biblical and theological studies of peacemaking, a background analysis of new global realities, and a number of specific recommendations for practical actions that individuals and congregations could take.

In the years that have followed, peacemaking has remained a major emphasis of Presbyterian faith and action. The annual collection of the Peacemaking Offering in October has provided millions of dollars for programs on the local, presbytery, and General Assembly level, and has enabled us to remain cognizant of the critical witness we must maintain in Christ's name. Every year the Congregational Ministries Division, through the work of the Presbyterian Peacemaking Program, distributes excellent study and worship materials for congregations to use with adults and children.

In the meetings of the General Assembly after 1983, peacemaking continued to be a major emphasis:

- In 1992 guidelines for dealing with conflict in the church were adopted, encouraging Presbyterians to work through periods of disagreement in a spirit of trust and love (See "Seeking to be Faithful Together: Guidelines for Presbyterians during Times of Disagreement").
- In 1995, recognizing the fiftieth anniversary of the conclusion of World War II, the 207th Assembly gave thanks for the extension of the Non-Proliferation Treaty, for the U.S. moratorium on nuclear testing, and for progress toward a comprehensive test ban, renewing the call of the church for a permanent end to the testing of nuclear weapons. These sentiments were reaffirmed the next year.
- In 1998 the 210th Assembly approved "Just Peacemaking and the Call for International Intervention for Humanitarian Rescue," providing a major analysis of the humanitarian, sociological, and theological ramifications of the post–Cold War era and reaffirming the theological convictions at the heart of the church's peacemaking commitment. Recognizing that some human disasters call for emergency response, even the use of military force, the study suggests guidelines for limited intervention that would preserve life as well as restrain or punish those responsible. It also calls powerfully for preventive diplomacy, "the taking of transforming initiatives" that can be applied to situations in order to prevent international violence and conflict. This is done in the hope that the "last resort" of military response may be avoided. The concept of "just peacemaking" is contrasted with that of a "just war," the former being far more limited than the latter, avoiding all-out conflict and utilizing military intervention only for humanitarian purposes or the use of armed forces in direct peacekeeping actions. In the future, this important distinction should urge Presbyterians to consider U.S. proposals critically that propose preemptive military strikes against nations that may be developing nuclear bombs or chemical and biological weapons. Are such strikes legal according to international law? Are they ethical, are they just, do they protect the lives of innocent civilians?

The 1998 report concludes on a note of limited optimism:

It is important to affirm confidence in the existence of a cosmic intentionality for human well-being. Peacemaking presupposes that God wills human well-being, that the divine sovereignty supports efforts to improve human conditions and human relationships. Peacemaking and peacekeeping (with all the military, political, social, and spiritual resources that are entailed) can only thrive on a conviction, through God's providential sovereignty, that as humans struggle for justice the world will move toward greater international harmony and profounder experiences of beneficial well-being than it has known in the past.[7]

Prospects: How Can the Text Be Rightly Used in the Future?

Planning for the last chapter of a book normally occurs months before the text is finally written. Ironically, I composed the concluding words of this chapter during the second week of September 2001, in the midst of the suffering, confusion, fear, and anger caused by the terrorist attacks on New York City and Washington, D.C., and the crash of the United Airlines flight in Pennsylvania. In the span of a few hours, the world seemed eerily different. At no time in recent memory has it been more clear to Presbyterians and all other American Christians that peacemaking is certainly our calling.

What can Christians do at such an ominous time? In the midst of the frightening reality of terrorist attacks on our own shore, with examples of great heroism being displayed, within hearing of the angry voices shouting for revenge and the indiscriminate destruction of real and imagined enemies, we must remain as close as possible to our Lord and maintain a prayerful sense of what he calls us to do.

No doubt we will all have ample opportunity over the next few years to carry out our responsibilities as spiritual leaders. Conversations will continue at work, in the schools, in grocery stores, colleges, seminaries, and church coffee hours, as we all ask how this could have happened, how it can be prevented in the future. As church members, pastors, and officers called by God to be ones who make peace, let us pray that we will be adequate to the task, so that everywhere we go we are able to bring spiritual wisdom and become the voices of sanity, moderation, forgiveness, and the love of Christ. In spite of the natural desire for revenge, Presbyterians must continue to provide a voice calling for measured responses, the taking of "transforming initiatives," and the prevention of carpet bombing techniques that indiscriminantly kill the innocent with the guilty.

Certainly we can all recommit ourselves to being peacemakers wherever we live or work. Churches can continue to take the annual Peacemaking Offering to fund creative efforts in the community and in the church to reach out to victims of violence, to families of prisoners, to those trapped by addiction, to children caged in poverty, to women who have suffered abuse, to single parents, and to those who suffer from religious persecution.

Congregations can work to send members to work on missionary projects in the United States and to other countries to help create international understanding on a spiritual and cultural level. When local leaders travel to countries in Africa or Asia, for example, and assist in the rebuilding of churches, schools, and hospitals, or contribute to the construction of low-cost housing, they do more than provide money and skills in short supply in developing nations. They also obey Christ's command to go into all the world and put God's love into visible and practical forms. When they work with Christians in other countries, they almost always get much more than they give. They do more than share what they have; they also bring back a new perspective of the world and benefit from the witness of believers who believe in Christ despite hardship, the privations of war, and poverty. The resulting fellowship of shared work and prayer creates bridges of joy and peace that can help make the world more stable and loving in the years to come.

We can endorse political candidates who support world community and look for solutions to common problems through negotiation and diplomacy rather than armed force.

We can resolve to make peacemaking a central part of Christian education, confident that if our children learn how to deal with conflict in constructive ways, they will acquire skills to enable them to live in a safer and saner world. As parents, we must talk to our children about peacemaking as seriously and as frequently as we do about telling the truth, studying in school, and saying "no" to drugs, so they can find a future that is free of fear, prejudice, oppression, and violence.

We can join with other Christians and other interfaith partners to try to understand the root causes of violence and work toward a day when economic and political freedom will be offered to all the people of the world. Presbyterians can continue to fight against poverty, battle injustice, and call for a more equitable distribution of wealth as we listen to cries of brothers and sisters at home and abroad whose needs are greater than our own. We can continue our commitment to a lifestyle that calls for sharing rather than accumulation, that encourages Christians to give more and keep less for themselves, that works for an economic environment that provides the basic necessities to all of God's children.

We could return to a concept advocated by past General Assemblies for the establishment of a United States Academy of Peace and Conflict Resolution (1980, UPCUSA; 1981, PCUS; 1983, PC(USA)). If we can support military academies for the Army, Air Force, and Navy so that soldiers can learn skills for military intervention and war, why not create a national peace academy where leaders can learn about conflict management, mediation, diplomacy, and peaceful intervention? The recent endorsement of the 214th General Assembly (2002) of a proposal to create a federal cabinet-level Department of Peace is also a step in the right direction.

We could work to endow chairs or departments of biblical peacemaking in our leading theological seminaries. The establishment of just one chair would make it possible to train peacemakers on a formal level before conflicts arise.

It would allow scholars, pastors, elders, and Christian politicians to study scriptural concepts of peacemaking, principles of negotiation, and nonviolent resistance on a master's and doctoral level within the tradition of Reformed theology. It would make it possible to create a cadre of peacemakers who would be available all over the globe to work on conflicts before they escalate into violence. Merely the establishment of such chairs would send a message to all future pastors and doctoral candidates that the seminary takes peacemaking very seriously, that it deserves a place of its own, rather than being subsumed under some other department. Seminary presidents and members of boards of trustees may think that such a step is too costly or not important enough to engage their attention or energy. But in a world filled with violence, how can we afford not to make the teaching of peacemaking a primary goal? When we consider the hundreds of thousands of dollars that local congregations invest in capital repairs and the amount that members spend to travel and purchase summer homes and boats, when we realize that for the price of two cruise missiles it would be possible to commit ourselves to Jesus' challenge to reach for the kingdom of heaven in a visible way by endowing such an academic chair, how can we continue to say that such a valuable step is too expensive or beyond our grasp?

Peacemaking can be our beginning or our end. It can be the call to worship and service in the years to come, or if we fail to embrace it fully, it can become our benediction and recessional. Future generations will not have to wait long to find out how serious we are about serving the God of Peace, the one who longs to make us complete in everything good, working among us that which is pleasing to God, through Jesus Christ, to whom be glory for ever and ever (Heb. 13:20–21).

Questions for Study and Reflection

1. Read my poem about Jesus and his ability to give us peace. Do you think that peacemaking is primarily an inner quality that a Christian has, or is it something that the believer does? Or is it both at once?

> Peace I leave with you
> My peace I give to you
> Be not troubled
> Neither be afraid.
>
> Is peace inside or out,
> Is it one thing or the other,
> To be at peace within,
> Or reconcile sister and brother?

Do we make tea
In leaves or the water?
Where does the brew reside
Without the two together?

Is making peace a prayer,
Quiet meditation,
Or is it active work,
Political participation?

How can Christ be inside
And infusing us with power
If we refuse to risk ourselves
To make the world taste stronger?

How can the mystery be true
That God in me is peace,
And that within God's peace I dwell?
Is God outside us, or with us, Emmanuel?[8]

2. In light of recent terrorist attacks around the world, especially those in American cities, how much more difficult is it to be a peacemaker? How will your neighbors react if you call for toleration or love of our enemies?
3. How important is it for you and other members of your congregation to study and critique U.S. policies in order to work for peace in the world?

Notes

INTRODUCTION

1. *Biblical Authority and Interpretation,* published by the Office of the General Assembly, PDS #70420-98-006, 1982. Republished in 1998 along with *Presbyterian Understanding and Use of Holy Scripture* (1983), 60.

2. See Bradley J. Longfield, *The Presbyterian Controversy: Fundamentalists, Modernists, and Moderates* (New York: Oxford University Press, 1991); Jack B. Rogers and Donald K. McKim, "Pluralism and Policy in Presbyterian Views of Scripture," in *The Confessional Mosaic: Presbyterians and Twentieth-Century Theology,* ed. Milton J. Coalter, John M. Mulder, and Louis B. Weeks (Louisville, Ky.: Westminster/John Knox Press, 1990), 37–58.

3. *Biblical Authority and Interpretation,* 37.

4. Oldenburg sent the challenge along with the previous General Assembly interpretations of the authority of the Bible. See note 1.

5. *Biblical Authority and Interpretation,* 60–61. See the discussion of these principles in Rogers and McKim, "Pluralism and Policy," 51–52, and in Jack Rogers, *Reading the Bible and the Confessions: The Presbyterian Way* (Louisville, Ky.: Geneva Press, 1999), 31–50. Reformed principles of interpreting the Bible are also discussed in Earl S. Johnson Jr., *Selected to Serve: A Guide for Church Officers* (Louisville, Ky.: Geneva Press, 2000), 120–24.

6. *Biblical Authority and Interpretation,* 34.

7. Ibid., 54–62.

8. *Presbyterian Understanding and Use,* 9.

9. "The Nature of Revelation in the Christian Tradition from a Reformed Perspective," in *Selected Theological Statements of the Presbyterian Church (U.S.A.) General Assemblies (1956–1998)* (Louisville, Ky.: Theology and Worship, Christian Faith and Life, Congregational Ministries Division, 1998), 385–407.

10. Ibid., 392.

11. Ibid., 393.

12. *Using the Bible: A Guided Study of Presbyterian Statements on Biblical Authority and Interpretation* (Louisville, Ky.: Theology and Worship Ministry Unit, Presbyterian Church (U.S.A.), 1993), DMS #277-92-101.

13. Ibid., 15, 60.

14. A more recent model for Bible study among those who disagree about basic issues of interpretation has been developed by Daniel Patte, *The Challenge of Discipleship: A Critical*

Study of the Sermon on the Mount as Scripture (Harrisburg, Pa: Trinity Press International, 1999).

15. Rogers, *Reading the Bible,* 124.

16. Ibid., 127.

17. For illustrations, see Rogers, *Reading the Bible,* 75, 77, 79, 120.

18. See James Smart, *The Strange Silence of the Bible in the Church: A Study in Hermeneutics* (Philadelphia: Westminster Press, 1970).

19. *Effective Christian Education: A National Study of Protestant Congregations. A Research Project of the Search Institute* (Minneapolis: The Search Institute, 1990), 34. A recent Gallup poll provides somewhat similar conclusions: 41 percent of those interviewed say that they "rarely or never" read the Bible, and only 16 percent read it "daily or more often." Although 65 percent of the respondents indicate that they believe the Bible "answers all or most of the basic questions of life," 86 percent of them are not involved in a Bible study group. (See gallup.com, "Gallup Poll Topic: A–Z, Bible.") Overall, readership of the Bible in the United States has declined from 73 percent in 1980 to 59 percent in 2000; see "Six in Ten Americans Read Bible at Least Occasionally—Percentage of Frequent Readers Has Decreased over Last Decade," October 20, 2000, gallup.com.

20. *Effective Christian Education,* 3; see also 11–17.

CHAPTER 1: JESUS IS LORD

1. See the comments of Martin Hengel, *Studies in Early Christianity* (Edinburgh: T. & T. Clark, 1995), 379–85.

2. To see how Paul interacts with imperial power, see Richard A. Horsley, ed., *Paul and Empire: Religion and Power in Roman Imperial Society* (Harrisburg, Pa.: Trinity Press International, 1997). See also the discussion and bibliographic references in Earl S. Johnson Jr., "Mark 5:1–20: The Other Side," *Irish Biblical Studies* 20 (1998): 50–74; and "Mark 15.39 and the So-Called Confession of the Roman Centurion," *Biblica* 81 (2000): 406–13.

3. See I. Howard Marshall, *The Origins of New Testament Christology,* updated ed. (Downers Grove, Ill: InterVarsity Press, 1990) 98–99, 106–8.

4. For a recent study of various views of the significance of this text, see Frank J. Matera, *New Testament Christology* (Louisville, Ky.: Westminster John Knox Press, 1999), 125–30. Cf. other New Testament passages with a high Christology (e.g., Rom. 1:4; 1 Cor. 1:3; 12:3; 2 Cor. 3:17; 13:4).

5. Joseph A. Fitzmyer, *Romans: A New Translation with Introduction and Commentary,* Anchor Bible (New York: Doubleday, 1993), 588.

6. R. H. Fuller, "Lord," in *Harper's Bible Dictionary,* ed. Paul J. Achtemeier (San Francisco: Harper & Row, 1985).

7. See Joseph A. Fitzmyer, "New Testament Kyrios and Maranatha and Their Aramaic Background," in *To Advance the Gospel: New Testament Studies* (New York: Crossroad, 1981). The evidence from Qumran and other sources is discussed more recently by Christopher Tuckett, *Christology and the New Testament: Jesus and His Earliest Followers* (Louisville, Ky.: Westminster John Knox Press, 2001), 19–22, 56–60.

8. *The Nature of the Church and the Practice of Governance, Approved by the 205th General Assembly (1993) Presbyterian Church (U.S.A.)* (Louisville, Ky.: Office of the General Assembly, 1993), 7. In the previous year, the General Assembly approved a statement about the Lordship of Jesus in reference to the question of abortion rights: "Do Justice, Love Mercy, Walk Humbly (Micah 6:8)," 204th General Assembly (1992), in *Selected Theological State-*

ments of the Presbyterian Church (U.S.A.) General Assemblies (Louisville, Ky.: Presbyterian Church (U.S.A.), 1998), 151–52.

9. Martin Luther, *A Commentary on St. Paul's Epistle to the Galatians*, trans. Phillip S. Watson (London: James Clarke and Co., 1961), 42–45.

10. John Calvin, *The First Epistle of Paul to the Corinthians*, trans. John W. Fraser, ed. David W. Torrance and Thomas F. Torrance (Grand Rapids: Wm. B. Eerdmans Publishing Co., 1960), 259.

11. We Presbyterians often use the expression "our Lord and Savior Jesus Christ," even though this combination of titles is rarely found in the New Testament—in fact, only in a few texts in 2 Peter.

12. See also the Heidelberg Catechism, Question 34 (C-4.034), and the Westminster Confession (C. 6.051; 6.184). For a recent discussion of the background of the *Book of Confessions*, see Johnson, *Selected to Serve*, 94–117.

13. "The Confessional Nature of the Church," General Assembly Minutes 1986, in *Selected Theological Statements*, 91.

14. "Turn to the Living God: A Call to Evangelism in Christ's Way," 203rd General Assembly, 1991, in *Selected Theological Statements*, 617–34.

15. Volunteers in Shared Ministry is part of the Worldwide Ministries Division of the General Assembly, and organizes mission projects nationally and internationally.

16. S.E.R.V.E. (Sending Experienced Retired Volunteers Everywhere), P.O. Box 284, Elverson, PA 19520 (610-286-1978), sponsors several mission expeditions annually for volunteers of all ages.

17. For summaries of this work, see Marcus J. Borg, *Jesus in Contemporary Scholarship* (Valley Forge, Pa.: Trinity Press International, 1994). For an assessment from a different perspective, see William R. Herzog II, *Jesus, Justice, and the Reign of God: A Ministry of Liberation* (Louisville, Ky.: Westminster John Knox Press, 2000).

18. See, for example, "The Search for Jesus," *Time,* April 8, 1996; "Rethinking the Resurrection: A New Debate about the Risen Christ," *Newsweek,* April 8, 1996; "Jesus at 2000," *Time,* December 6, 1999; "Visions of Jesus: How Jews, Muslims, and Buddhists View Him," *Newsweek,* March 27, 2000. See also "2000 Years of Christianity: The Meaning of the Millennium," *Life,* December 1999; "The First Christians: A Fresh Look at Christianity's Turbulent Early Days," *U.S. News and World Report,* April 20, 1992.

19. A good example, which is excellent for stimulating discussion, is *Jesus,* starring Jeremy Sisto, Debra Messing, and Jacqueline Bisset, produced by Paolo Piria and Russell Kagan for Five Mile Films (Trimark Home Video, 1999).

20. In addition to the Covenant Network of Presbyterians and the Presbyterian Coalition, conservatives have formed a national Confessing Church Movement, and liberals have created a new Auburn Affirmation called "Affirmation 2001." For background and analysis, see John H. Adams, "Evangelicals Rally behind Confessing Church Movement," *The Presbyterian Layman,* April 2001, 1–2; "3 Conservative Credos Fuel Confessing 'Movement,'" *The News, Presbyterian Church (U.S.A.),* April 27, 2001, 5; William Stacey Johnson, "Confessional Wellness and Its Challenge," *Presbyterian Outlook,* May 14, 2001; William Stacey Johnson, "Equally Yoked," *Presbyterian Outlook,* May 28, 2001. The first core tenet of the Confessing Movement is "Jesus Christ alone is Lord of all and the way of salvation."

21. Ficca's speech is available at http://horeb.pcusa.org/peacemaking/ficca.htm.

22. For reactions, see "The Jesus Debate ("What is the big deal about Jesus?"), www.presbyweb.com/JesusDebateIndex.htm. See also A. J. McKelway, "Reflections on Dirk Ficca's Speech," *Presbyterian Outlook,* April 16, 2001, 6–7. In May 2001 the Presbyterian church in

Montreat, N.C., filed a remedial case against the GAC for failing to coordinate and review the work of the Peacemaking unit, contending that the very fabric of the Presbyterian system was at stake. See Leslie Scanlon, "Montreat Church to File Complaint against GAC," *Presbyterian Outlook,* June 11, 2001, 3.

23. "Presentation to His Holiness, John Paul II, on Behalf of the Delegation from the Presbyterian Church (U.S.A.)," an Internet link in Jerry L. Van Marter, "Presbyterians Travel to the Vatican in Search of Unity with Roman Catholics," *Presbyterian News Service,* March 27, 2001, 01106. A link to the joint statement is also found in Van Marter's article. See also "GAC Affirms Lordship of Christ, Defends 'Open Dialogue' in Conferences," *The News, Presbyterian Church (U.S.A.),* March 9, 2001, 5–6. "Successor to Peter" is available online from the Office of the General Assembly, www.pcusa.org/oga/OGA%20news/Peter.pdf.

24. "Turn to the Living God," 625.

25. *Building Community among Strangers: A Report on Racism, Social Class Division, Sex-Based Injustices, Religious Intolerance, and Conflict, Approved by the 211th General Assembly (1999)* (Louisville, Ky.: Office of the General Assembly Presbyterian Church (U.S.A.) PDS #OGA-99-028, 1999). For further suggestions, see Earl S. Johnson,Jr., *Selected to Serve,* 74–76. See also the excellent guidelines for protocol and prayer at interfaith meetings and services of worship in "Handbook for Ecumenical and Interfaith Relations" (Louisville, Ky.: Global Mission Ministry Unit, Office of Ecumenical and Interfaith Relations, 1992). The September 11, 2001, terrorist attacks on the United States opened up increased interest in interfaith dialogue, and many memorial services held thereafter included clergy from several different faiths.

26. For suggestions from different points of view, see Eva Stimpson, "Don't Dodge the Jesus Debate," *Presbyterians Today,* January/February 2001, 2; Cynthia L. Rigby, "Jesus Is the Way: Presbyterian Theology Affirms the Uniqueness of Christ," *Presbyterians Today,* April 2001, 15–17; editorials in the *Presbyterian Outlook* by Robert Bullock Jr., "Jesus Christ: An Apology," October 9, 2000; "A Testimony," October 16, 2000; "Jesus the Theologian: Salt and Light," (October 28–30, 2000); "Confession," November 6, 2000; "Life," November 13, 2000.

27. "Confessional Nature of the Church," 92.

CHAPTER 2: JUSTIFICATION BY FAITH ALONE

1. "Preface to the Complete Edition of Luther's Latin Writings," in *Martin Luther: Selections from His Writings,* ed. John Dillenberger (Garden City, N.Y.: Anchor Books, 1961), 11.

2. John Calvin, *Institutes of the Christian Religion,* ed. John T. McNeill, trans. Ford Lewis Battles (Philadelphia: Westminster Press, 1960), 3.11.1.

3. Eberhard Busch, *Karl Barth: His Life from Letters and Autobiographical Texts,* trans. John Bowden (Philadelphia: Fortress Press, 1976), 266.

4. Quoted in Busch, *Karl Barth,* 98.

5. Paul does not cite the Old Testament text from either the Hebrew or the Greek version (Septuagint) but probably recites it either from memory or from a version of Habakkuk no longer available. See Ernest Best, *The Letter of Paul to the Romans,* Cambridge Bible Commentary of the New English Bible (Cambridge: Cambridge University Press, 1967), 17.

6. See A. J. M. Wedderburn, *The Reasons for Romans* (Minneapolis: Fortress Press, 1991).

7. For discussions of Paul's interaction and conflict with Roman imperial power, emperor worship, and the political policies of Rome, see the essays in *Paul and Empire: Religion and*

Power in Roman Imperial Society, ed. Richard A. Horsley (Harrisburg, Pa.: Trinity Press International, 1997).

8. For a recent detailed discussion of Paul's purposes in writing and the history of interpretation of Romans, see Joseph Fitzmyer, *Romans: A New Translation with Introduction and Commentary,* Anchor Bible (New York: Doubleday, 1993), 68–80.

9. See "Justification," in *Harper's Bible Dictionary,* ed. Paul J. Achtemeier (San Francisco: Harper & Row, 1985), 520.

10. See Van A. Harvey, *A Handbook of Theological Terms* (New York: Macmillan, 1964), 135.

11. C. H. Dodd, *The Epistle of Paul to the Romans* (London and Glasgow: Fontana Books, 1963), 80.

12. "Faith," in *A Theological Word Book of the Bible,* ed. Alan Richardson (New York: Macmillan, 1975), 75.

13. Best, *Letter of Paul to the Romans,* 17.

14. Ibid.

15. Martin Luther was often accused of adding the word "alone" to Paul's text, but he defended its use in his translation (*allyn*) because it was demanded by the context and had been used by commentators before him (*sola fides*). See Fitzmyer's detailed discussion of the tradition of this interpretation before Luther in *Romans,* 360–62. As Fitzmyer points out, it is ironic that the closest parallel in the New Testament to Luther's translation is found in a text he did not particularly like—James 2:24.

16. For detailed commentaries on Galatians, see Earl S. Johnson Jr., *Galatians and Ephesians,* Basic Bible Commentary (Nashville: Abingdon Press, 1994); Ronald Y. K. Fung, *The Epistle to the Galatians,* New International Commentary on the New Testament (Grand Rapids: Wm. B. Eerdmans Publishing Co., 1988); Richard D. Longenecker, *Galatians,* Word Biblical Commentary (Dallas: Word, 1990); Ben Witherington III, *Grace in Galatia: A Commentary on Paul's Letter to the Galatians* (Grand Rapids: Wm. B. Eerdmans Publishing Co., 1998).

17. The contrast between Paul's teaching on justification by faith (alone) and James's insistence that faith without works is dead (Jas. 2:17) is often noted. Is James trying to jettison the concept of salvation through grace, or is he reacting to a kind of theology that had focused too much on Paul's emphasis on freedom by withdrawing into a passive type of faith that was not reaching out to others enough in the name of Christ? Or is it possible that he represents the viewpoint of Jewish Christians who refused to give up the observance of law (see Matt. 5:17) even though they still believed in Jesus? For possibilities, see Earl S. Johnson Jr., *James; First and Second Peter; First, Second, and Third John; and Jude,* Basic Bible Commentary (Nashville: Abingdon Press, 1994), esp. 9–10, 27–30. See also discussions by John Calvin, *Institutes,* 3.17.11, and in the Second Helvetic Confession (C-5.111).

18. "Preface to Romans," in Dillenberger, ed., *Martin Luther,* 23–25.

19. For studies of the *Book of Confessions,* see Johnson, *Selected to Serve,* 94–117; Rogers, *Presbyterian Creeds;* Harry W. Eberts Jr., *We Believe: A Study of the Book of Confessions for Church Officers* (Philadelphia: Geneva Press, 1987); Rogers, *Reading the Bible.*

20. See *Book of Order,* appendix C, "A Formula of Agreement."

21. Peggy Polk, "Vatican Declares Only the Roman Catholic Church Brings Salvation," *Religion News Service,* reported by *Presbyterian News Service,* September 7, 2000, 00321.

22. Peggy Polk, "Catholic, Lutheran, and Reformed Churches Discuss Indulgences," *Religion News Service,* reported by *Presbyterian News Service,* February 26, 2001, 01078.

23. "Presentation to His Holiness, John Paul II on Behalf of the Delegation from the Presbyterian Church (U.S.A.)," an Internet link in Jerry L. Van Marter, "Presbyterians Travel

to the Vatican in Search of Unity with Roman Catholics," *Presbyterian News Service,* March 27, 2001, 01106. A link to the joint statement is also found in Van Marter's article. Also see "GAC Affirms Lordship of Christ, Defends 'Open Dialogue' in Conferences," *The News, Presbyterian Church (U.S.A.),* March 9, 2001, 5–6. "Successor to Peter" is available online from the Office of the General Assembly, www.pcusa.org/oga/OGA%20news/Peter.pdf.

24. Heiko A. Oberman, *Luther: Man between God and the Devil* (New Haven, Conn.: Yale University Press, 1989), 323.

25. Ibid., 324.

26. Ibid., 330.

27. John Leith, *Basic Christian Doctrine* (Louisville, Ky.: Westminster/John Knox Press, 1993), 180.

28. Calvin, *Institutes,* 3.12.8. Calvin discusses justification by faith and the grace of Christ at great length in book 3, chapters 11–19.

29. Robert Jewett, *Paul the Apostle to America: Cultural Trends and Pauline Scholarship* (Louisville, Ky.: Westminster John Knox Press, 1994), 87–97.

30. Ibid., 96.

31. Elsa Tamez, *The Amnesty of Grace: Justification by Faith from a Latin American Perspective,* trans. Sharon H. Ringe (Nashville: Abingdon Press, 1993). For further study, see Tamez's *The Scandalous Message of James: Faith without Works Is Dead,* trans. John Eagleson (New York: Crossroad, 1992).

CHAPTER 3: IN THE BEGINNING

1. "Evolution and the Bible," in *Selected Theological Statements,* 174–75.

2. The Hebrew text allows itself to be translated either way. Everett Fox selects a third alternative, "At the beginning of God's creating of the heavens and the earth," in *The Five Books of Moses* (New York: Schocken Books, 1995).

3. This date was proposed by Archbishop James Ussher (1580–1656). See Lloyd R. Bailey, *Genesis, Creation, and Creationism* (Mahwah, N.J.: Paulist Press, 1993), 121, 199–200.

4. See Gordon J. Wenham, *Genesis 1–15,* Word Biblical Commentary (Waco, Tex.: Word, 1987), 5–6; Terence E. Fretheim, "The Book of Genesis," in *The New Interpreter's Bible* (Nashville: Abingdon Press, 1994), 322, 340.

5. See Fretheim, *Book of Genesis,* 328–30, 340.

6. See Richard J. Clifford, *Creation Accounts in the Ancient Near East and in the Bible,* Catholic Biblical Quarterly Monograph Series 24 (Washington, D.C.: Catholic Biblical Association, 1994); Fretheim, *Book of Genesis,* 341; Walter Brueggemann, *Genesis,* Interpretation: A Bible Commentary for Teaching and Preaching (Atlanta: John Knox Press, 1982), 25.

7. Fretheim, *Book of Genesis,* 337 (see also 341), calls the perspectives of the editors of Genesis "pre-scientific."

8. Note the persistent use of noninclusive language in modern translations when the point clearly is that the image of God reflects both female and male qualities. Elizabeth Cady Stanton, a Presbyterian originally from Johnstown, N.Y., was truly ahead of her time when she wrote, "If language has any meaning, we have in these texts a plain declaration of the existence of the feminine element in the God-head, equal in power and glory with the masculine. The Heavenly Mother and Father!" (*The Woman's Bible* [Amherst, N.Y.: Prometheus Books, 1999], 14).

9. For other interpretations of God's image, see Brueggemann, *Genesis,* 28, 33–35, especially in relation to New Testament usage.

10. *Restoring Creation for Ecology and Justice: A Report Adopted by the 202nd General*

Assembly (1990) Presbyterian Church (U.S.A.) (Louisville, Ky.: Office of the General Assembly, 1990), 106–7.

11. Reviews of Presbyterian environmental statements are found in *Presbyterian Social Witness Policy Compilation, Presbyterian Church (U.S.A.) and Its Antecedents, Presbyterian Church in the U.S. and the United Presbyterian Church in the U.S.A. 1946–1999* (Louisville, Ky.: Advisory Committee on Social Witness Policy of the General Assembly, 2000), 225–53. See also *Restoring Creation for Ecology and Justice,* 33–42.

12. *Keeping and Healing the Creation* (Louisville, Ky.: Committee on Social Witness Policy Presbyterian Church (U.S.A.) 1989).

13. *Hope for a Global Future: Toward Just and Sustainable Human Development,* approved by the 208th General Assembly (1996) Presbyterian Church (U.S.A.) (Louisville, Ky.: Presbyterian Distribution Service, 1996). A discussion of the Genesis creation narratives is found on 59–67.

14. *Hope for a Global Future,* 81. *Church and Society* (a journal published by the National Ministries Division, Presbyterian Church (U.S.A.)) has devoted a number of volumes on ecojustice issues. See the articles in July-August 1996, *For the Beauty of the Earth: Restoring Creation for Ecology and Justice;* January-February 1997, *Hope for a Global Future: Toward Just and Sustainable Human Development;* September-October 1998, *Global Ethics: On the Threshold of a New Millennium.* For study and liturgical resources to use in the church, see Vera K. White, *Healing and Defending God's Creation: Hands On! Practical Ideas for Congregations,* vol. 2 (Louisville, Ky.: Presbyterian Church (U.S.A.)), DMS #259-93-939.

15. Those working to preserve the environment through political means face a difficult task. The Bush administration does not support the Kyoto Protocol, and on July 23, 2001, after three days of nonstop negotiations, 178 nations reached a climate accord that the United States refused to endorse. Although the United States sent a climate report to the United Nations in June, 2002 that outlines the future danger of global warming, the administration recommends adaptations to radical environmental changes, rather than the active reduction of the greenhouse gases responsible for causing them. In July 2002, the attorneys general of eleven states wrote the president, urging the passage of federal regulations to limit emissions.

16. The discussion is constantly before the public, especially on a popular level. See the information provided, for example, in the special issue of *Time,* "Earth Day 2000," Spring 2000, especially Eugene Linden, "State of the Planet: Condition Critical," 18–24. See also Jeffrey Kluger, "Global Warming: A Climate for Despair," *Time,* April 9, 2001, 30–36.

17. Bill McKibben, "Climate Change and the Unraveling of Creation," *Christian Century,* December 8, 1999, 1197. See also "A Conversation with Bill McKibben," *Alive Now!,* July-August, 2000, 28–33; *The End of Nature,* 10th anniversary ed. with a new introduction (New York: Doubleday, 1999).

18. McKibben, "Climate Change," 1199. In a recent study of the Pacific Island of Nauru, Carl N. McDaniel and John M. Gowdy illustrate how current first-world economic policies are destroying the fabric of nature. See their *Paradise for Sale: A Parable of Nature* (Berkeley Calif.: University of California Press, 2000).

19. See the essays in John P. Burgess, ed., *In Whose Image? Faith, Science, and the New Genetics* (Louisville, Ky.: Geneva Press, 1998), especially R. David Cole, "Do Genes Control Us?" 53–72; I. Lehr Brisbin Jr., "Perspectives on the Origins and Evolution of Humanity: In Whose Image Are We Really Made?" 73–89. See also Evan Silverstein, "The Genetics Revolution: Medical Marvels Raise Moral and Ethical Questions," *Presbyterians Today,* October 2001, 10–16. The article contains a summary of General Assembly responses to recent biological research since 1990.

20. Roger Rosenblatt, "Why Protecting the Environment Means Saving Ourselves All the Days of the Earth," *Time,* Spring 2000, special ed., *Earth Day 2000,* 15.

21. Richard Leakey, "Extinctions Past and Present," *Time,* Spring 2000, 35.

22. For a detailed description of the background of creationism, see Lloyd R. Bailey, *Genesis, Creation, and Creationism* (Mahwah, N.J.: Paulist Press, 1993). See a recent discussion of the Genesis text on a popular level by Marcus J. Borg, *Reading the Bible Again for the First Time: Taking the Bible Seriously but Not Literally* (San Francisco: HarperSanFrancisco, 2001).

23. Daniel L. Migliore, "The Ecological Crisis and the Doctrine of Creation," *Princeton Theological Seminary Bulletin* 12, no. 3 (1991): 282.

24. See Migliore, "Ecological Crisis," 277–82.

25. See, for example, the stimulating work of Sallie McFague, *The Body of God: An Ecological Theology* (Minneapolis: Fortress Press, 1993).

26. "A new cosmic christology must end the historic christology of modern times, not abolishing it but gathering it into something more, which will overcome its limitations and preserve its truth" (Jürgen Moltmann, *Jesus Christ for Today's World,* trans. Margaret Kohl [Minneapolis: Fortress Press, 1994], 89).

27. Holmes Rolston III, "The Bible and Ecology," *Interpretation,* January 1996, 19. See the other excellent articles in the same issue, *Theology and Ecology,* by James A. Nash, W. Sibley Towner, and Theodore Hiebert.

CHAPTER 4: THOSE PREDESTINED WERE ALSO CALLED

1. See Walter L. Lingle and John W. Kuykendall, *Presbyterians and Their Beliefs* (Atlanta: John Knox Press, 1988), 102.

2. The noninclusive language is Calvin's. For the background of this concept in pre-Reformation theology, especially in Augustine, see Calvin, *Institutes,* 3.21.1, note 1. Calvin argues elsewhere that God determined what was to be done with the whole human race before Adam and Eve were even created; see his "Articles concerning Predestination" in *Calvin: Theological Treatises,* trans. J. K. S. Reid, Library of Christian Classics (Philadelphia: Westminster Press, 1954), 178–80.

3. "Confessional Nature of the Church," 102–3.

4. See the essays by Edward Dowey in *Handbook of Christian Theology: Definition Essays on Concepts and Movements of Thought in Contemporary Protestantism,* ed. Marvin Halverson and Arthur A. Cohen (Cleveland: World Publishing Co., 1958), "Calvinism," 40–43; "Predestination," 271–72. The quotation is from "Calvinism," 41.

5. See Albert Curry Winn, "What Is the Gospel?" in *How Shall We Witness? Faithful Evangelism in a Reformed Tradition,* ed. Milton J. Coalter and Virgil Cruz (Louisville, Ky.: Westminster John Knox Press, 1995), 20.

6. Details of the debate are discussed by Lefferts A. Loetscher in *The Broadening Church: A Study of Theological Issues in the Presbyterian Church since 1869* (Philadelphia: University of Pennsylvania Press, 1954), 39–47, 81–89.

7. The charges against Charles A. Briggs of Union Theological Seminary in New York and Henry Preserved Smith of Lane Theological Seminary largely involved questions about their use of the principles of higher criticism in interpreting the Bible. See Loetscher, *Broadening Church,* 48–82; Longfield, *Presbyterian Controversy.*

8. James H. Smylie, *A Brief History of the Presbyterians* (Louisville, Ky.: Geneva Press, 1996), 99.

9. For detailed studies of the biblical concept of predestination, see I. H. Marshall, "Predestination in the New Testament," in *Jesus the Saviour* (Downers Grove, Ill: InterVarsity Press, 1990), 290–305; Benjamin Breckinridge Warfield, *Biblical and Theological Studies,* ed. Samuel G. Craig (Philadelphia: Presbyterian and Reformed Publishing Co., 1952), 270–333.

10. For a discussion of the nature of the call, not only to pastors and church officers but to all believers, see Johnson, *Selected to Serve,* 1–5.

11. Ernest Best, *Ephesians,* International Critical Commentary. (Edinburgh: T. & T. Clark, 1998), 123–24, 127.

12. Warfield, *Biblical and Theological Studies,* 271.

13. Leslie D. Weatherhead, a British preacher who was popular with pastors and church members in the 1940s and 1950s, argued that when an effort is made to determine the will of God in the world it is necessary to distinguish between God's "intentional will" (the ideal purpose), God's "circumstantial will" (often changed by conditions in the world), and God's "ultimate will" (the purposefulness of God that finally arrives, in spite of evil, with nothing of value lost). See his *The Will of God* (Nashville: Abingdon Press, 1972).

CHAPTER 5: LET MY PEOPLE GO

1. *The Presbyterian Hymnal* (Louisville, Ky.: Westminster/John Knox Press, 1990), 334. For a discussion of the background of this spiritual, see Lindajo H. McKim, *The Presbyterian Hymnal Companion* (Louisville, Ky.: Westminster/John Knox Press, 1993), 237.

2. Everett Fox, *The Five Books of Moses: Genesis, Exodus, Leviticus, Numbers, and Deuteronomy. A New Translation with Introduction, Commentary, and Notes* (New York: Schocken Books, 1995).

3. See also W-7.3000–7.5000 and the Confession of 1967, (C-9.17, 44–47).

4. See, for example, Kevin G. O'Connell, "Exodus," in *Harper's Bible Dictionary,* ed., Paul J. Achtemeier (San Francisco: Harper & Row, 1985); P. Kyle McCarter, "Exodus," in *Harper's Bible Commentary,* ed. James L. Mays (San Francisco: Harper & Row, 1988).

5. See Walter Brueggemann, "Exodus," in *The New Interpreter's Bible,* vol. 1 (Nashville: Abingdon Press, 1999), 681–83. See also the general articles in part 3 of the same volume, "How the Bible is Read, Interpreted, and Used," 33–212.

6. Brueggemann, "Exodus," 678–79.

7. Ibid., 679.

8. Ibid., 685.

9. The use of Babylon as a symbol for Rome is found in 1 Pet. 5:13 and in Rev. 14:8. The reinterpretation of the exodus theme is found in several places in the New Testament, notably in Matt. 5–7 (the Sermon on the Mount); Luke 6:12–49 (the Sermon on the Plain); 1 Cor. 10:1–13; Heb. 3–4.

10. *Records of the Presbyterian Church in the United States of America, Embracing the Minutes of the General Presbytery and General Synod, 1706–1788* (Philadelphia: Presbyterian Board of Publication and Sabbath-School Work, 1904; reprint, New York: Arno Press, 1969), 539.

11. In Roman law, property given to a slave to hold as his or her own possession.

12. *Records of the Presbyterian Church,* 540.

13. See Archie Crouch, "Racial-Ethnic Ministry Policies: An Historical Overview," *Journal of Presbyterian History* 57 (1979): 284. Crouch provides a valuable time line beginning in 1562 and including the colonial period.

14. Crouch, "Racial-Ethnic Ministry Policies," 285.

15.   Lefferts A. Loetscher, *A Brief History of the Presbyterians*, rev. and enlarged (Philadelphia: Westminster Press, 1958), 76–77. See also James H. Smylie, *A Brief History of the Presbyterians* (Louisville, Ky.: Geneva Press, 1996), 78.

16.   James Hastings Nichols, *Presbyterianism in New York State: A History of the Synod and its Predecessors* (Philadelphia: Westminster Press, 1963), 122–27.

17.   See Nichols, *Presbyterianism in New York State,* 126–33, for a detailed discussion of the proceedings.

18.   Nichols, *Presbyterianism in New York State,* 137. For a detailed examination of the differences between the two churches, see Harold M. Parker Jr., *The United Synod of the South: The Southern New School Presbyterian Church* (New York: Greenwood Press, 1988), 1–24.

19.   Earl and Elinore Johnson, *The History of First Presbyterian Church, Williamson, New York, 1816–2000* (Williamson, N.Y.: First Presbyterian Church, 2000), 10.

20.   *A Digest of the General Assembly Proceedings, Presbyterian Church U.S., 1861–1944, Authorized by the General Assembly* (Richmond: Presbyterian Committee on Publication, 1945), 33.

21.   Ibid., 36.

22.   Ibid., 38.

23.   Jack Rogers, *Reading the Bible and the Confessions,* 73–77, fails to appreciate the sophistication of the argument developed by the PCCSA when he contends that the Assembly relied on prooftexts to warrant their actions (see especially p. 75). Although the theory of the unity of Scripture and its inerrancy is clearly visible, the authors of the Assembly's statement developed a careful analysis of the interrelation of texts that goes far beyond a simple use of proof-texting.

24.   *Digest of the General Assembly Proceedings,* 38.

25.   Ibid., 39.

26.   Ibid., 37.

27.   Ibid., 39. Today we might use the Reformers and the testimony of the *Book of Confessions* to buttress our own conclusions.

28.   *Digest of the General Assembly Proceedings,* 42. In 1864, after years of bloody fighting and reverses, the Assembly took a much more strident position: "We hesitate not to confirm that it is the peculiar mission of the Southern church to conserve the institution of slavery and to make it a blessing both to master and slave" (161).

29.   See James O. Boswell III, *Slavery, Segregation, and Scripture* (Grand Rapids: Wm. B. Eerdmans Publishing Co., 1964), 12–18.

30.   *Digest of the General Assembly Proceedings,* 34.

31.   Theodore Dwight Weld, *The Bible against Slavery, or An Inquiry into the Genius of the Teachings of the Mosaic System, and the Teachings of the Old Testament on the Subject of Human Rights* (Detroit: Negro History Press, 1970).

32.   Ibid., iv.

33.   Ibid., 13.

34.   Ibid., 17.

35.   Ibid., 19.

36.   Ibid., 20–21.

37.   Weld argues on the basis of the prevailing understanding of the Mosaic authorship of the Pentateuch.

38.   Weld, *Bible against Slavery,* 62. Weld realizes that the conditions under which people might become slaves in the ancient world were complex and that the Old Testament presents situations that were quite different in nature. For recent studies, see Gregory C. Chirichigno,

Debt-Slavery in Israel and the Ancient Near East, Journal for the Study of the Old Testament: Supplement Series 141 (Sheffield: Sheffield Academic Press, 1993); I. A. H. Combes, *The Metaphor of Slavery in the Writings of the Early Church: From the New Testament to the Beginning of the Fifth Century,* Journal for the Study of the New Testament: Supplement Series 156 (Sheffield: Sheffield Academic Press, 1998).

39. Weld, *Bible against Slavery,* 149–54, esp. 152.

40. The importance of this passage in the debate is demonstrated by Weld's discussion of it and related texts in the remainder of his work *Bible against Slavery,* 95–147.

41. Weld, *Bible against Slavery,* 94.

42. The chronology of the mission efforts of the two churches is found in Crouch, "Racial-Ethnic Ministry Policies," 290–91.

43. See Douglas Bax, "The Bible and Apartheid 2," in *Apartheid Is a Heresy,* ed. John W. DeGrucy and Charles Villa-Vincencio (Grand Rapids: Wm. B. Eerdmans Publishing Co., 1987), 94–111.

44. See J. A. Loubser, *A Critical Review of Racial Theology in South Africa: The Apartheid Bible* (Lewiston, N.Y.: Edwin Mellen Press, 1987).

45. Loubser, *Critical Review of Racial Theology,* 25.

46. Ibid., 33–40.

47. Ibid., 106.

48. Willem Vorster, "The Bible and Apartheid 1," in *Apartheid Is a Heresy,* ed. John W. DeGrucy and Charles Villa-Vincencio (Grand Rapids: Wm. B. Eerdmans Publishing Co., 1987), 97, 98.

49. Ibid., 99–100.

50. See *The Kairos Document: Challenge to the Church, A Theological Comment on the Political Crisis in South Africa* (Grand Rapids: Wm. B. Eerdmans Publishing Co., 1986).

51. For other theological critiques of apartheid, see Charles Villa-Vincencio, *The Theology of Apartheid* (Cape Town: Methodist Publishing House, 1977), and the essays in *On Reading Karl Barth in South Africa,* ed. Charles Villa-Vincencio (Grand Rapids: Wm. B. Eerdmans Publishing Co., 1988).

52. "Presbyterian Theology, Policy, and Witness regarding South Africa," in *Minutes of the General Assembly,* Part I, *Journal* (New York and Atlanta: Office of the General Assembly, 1985), 27.221.

53. See the essays in *A Long Struggle: The Involvement of the World Council of Churches in South Africa,* ed. Pauline Webb (Geneva: WCC Publications, 1994).

54. "Divestment for South Africa: An Investment in Hope," in *Minutes of the General Assembly* (1985), Part I, *Journal,* 27.206.

55. *Minutes of the General Assembly,* Part I, *Journal* (New York: Office of the General Assembly, 1983), 445.

56. *Minutes of the General Assembly* (1985), Part I, *Journal,* 78. This action had been particularly urged by the South African Council of Churches and its general secretary, Bishop Desmond Tutu. During the period from 1972 to 1984, the Presbyterian Church (U.S.A.) had approached corporations in South Africa forty-nine times, requesting new economic and employment policies (p. 216).

57. *Minutes of the General Assembly* (1985), Part I, *Journal,* 218. According to a survey about the Presbyterian Church's call for corporate withdrawal, 44 percent of members, 49 percent of elders, and 81 percent of clergy said they agreed with the policy.

58. See *Minutes of the General Assembly,* Part I, *Journal,* (New York and Atlanta: Office of the General Assembly, 1987), 227, 231. The General Assembly also endorsed the Lusaka

Statement made by representatives of churches, trade unions, women's, youth, and anti-apartheid groups from South Africa.

59. See Donna Katzin, "Economic Strategies: An Evolving Prophetic Partnership between South African and US Churches," in *A Long Struggle: The Involvement of the World Council of Churches in South Africa* (Geneva: WCC Publications, 1994), 58–68.

60. Desmond Tutu, "Address to Deacons," in *Hope and Suffering, Sermons and Speeches,* comp. Mothobi Mutloatse, ed. John Webster (Grand Rapids: Wm. B. Eerdmans Publishing Co., 1984), 86.

61. For information on the use of divestment by other churches, see *Minutes of the General Assembly* (1985), Part I, *Journal,* 220–21.

62. Nelson Mandela, *The Long Walk to Freedom* (Boston: Little, Brown & Co., 1994), 624.

63. See, for example, the studies of James O. Boswell III, *Slavery, Segregation, and Scripture* (Grand Rapids: Wm. B. Eerdmans Publishing Co., 1964), and T. B. Maston, *The Bible and Race* (Nashville: Broadman Press, 1959).

64. Boswell, *Slavery, Segregation, and Scripture,* 52–53.

65. These arguments are carefully summarized in a recent book by Steven L. McKenzie, *All God's Children: A Biblical Critique of Racism* (Louisville, Ky.: Westminster John Knox Press, 1997). He also analyzes several other biblical texts used to defend racist practices.

66. This interpretation of Romans 13 draws particularly on the work of Allan A. Boesak, "What Belongs to Caesar? Once Again Romans 13," in *When Prayer Makes News,* ed. Allan A. Boesak and Charles Villa-Vincencio (Philadelphia: Westminster Press, 1986), 138–56.

67. Chronological information about the UPCUSA is found in Crouch, "Racial-Ethnic Ministry Policies," 272–303, unless otherwise indicated.

68. Information about the policies of the PCUS is found in *Presbyterian Social Witness Policy Compilation, Presbyterian Church (U.S.A.) and Its Antecedents, Presbyterian Church in the U.S. and the United Presbyterian Church in the U.S.A. 1946–1999* (Louisville, Ky.: Advisory Committee on Social Witness Policy, 2000).

69. *Journal of the 177th General Assembly,* Part I, the United Presbyterian Church in the United States of America (Philadelphia: Office of the General Assembly, 1965), 394–402.

70. *Journal of the 178th General Assembly,* Part I, the United Presbyterian Church in the United States of America (Philadelphia: Office of the General Assembly, 1966), 418–19.

71. *Journal of the 177th General Assembly* (1965), Part I, 406, 409.

72. In partial response, the General Assembly UPCUSA (1966) approved the pronouncement, "Segregation and Discrimination in Housing." It calls upon congregations and the housing industry to examine both conscience and conduct in the encouragement of residential integration by refusing to discriminate in the selling or renting of housing, by supporting groups organized for the purpose of seeking black buyers in white areas, and to encourage whites to move into black areas. See *Journal of the 179th General Assembly,* the United Presbyterian Church in the United States of America (Philadelphia: Office of the General Assembly, 1967), 337.

73. *Minutes of the General Assembly* (1983), Part I, *Journal,* 460–71.

74. *Minutes of the General Assembly* (1983), Part I, *Journal,* 466. For discussion of actions of the PC(USA) General Assembly in subsequent years, see *Presbyterian Social Witness Policy Compilation,* chapter 8, "Race and the Rights of Minorities in America," 295–322.

75. Desmond Tutu, "Your Policies Are Unbiblical, Unchristian, Immoral, and Evil," in *The Rainbow People of God: The Making of a Peaceful Revolution,* ed. John Allen (New York: Doubleday, 1994), 147.

76. Virgile Ahissou, "Benin Officials Say Child Trafficking Confirmed," *Schenectady Gazette,* May 1, 2001, A7.

77. The 213th General Assembly (2001) approved a commissioner's resolution confessing the corporate guilt of the PC(USA) in complicity in the evils of slavery. It also committed the church to working with African Americans to overcome the economic and social vestiges of slavery that still exist in the United States.

78. Vachel Lindsay, "The Unpardonable Sin," in *Chapters into Verse: Poetry in English Inspired by the Bible,* vol.2, *Gospels to Revelation,* ed. Robert Atwan and Laurance Wieder (Oxford: Oxford University Press, 1993), 93.

CHAPTER 6: NO LONGER MALE AND FEMALE

1. Elizabeth Cady Stanton and Susan B. Anthony, *The History of Woman Suffrage,* vol. 3 (Manchester, N.H.: Ayer Company, 1979).

2. Kathryn Cullen-Dupont, *Elizabeth Cady Stanton and Women's Liberty* (New York: Facts on File, 1992), 4–5.

3. Elizabeth Cady Stanton, *The Woman's Bible* (Amherst, N.Y.: Prometheus Books, 1999). For comments on her experiences in the Presbyterian sabbath school, see her *Eighty Years and More: Reminiscences 1815–1897* (Boston: Northeastern University Press, 1993), 111–12.

4. Stanton, *Woman's Bible,* 1213.

5. Other interpretations of Paul's attitude toward women also exist. Some commentators think that his more patriarchal statements reflect his true evaluation. Others suggest that he really was a misogynist. A third view is that his opinions were not consistent and cannot be reconciled. For a popular discussion of this debate, see John Temple Bristow, *What Paul Really Said about Women: An Apostle's Liberating Views on Equality in Marriage, Leadership, and Love* (San Francisco: Harper & Row, 1988). Brister thinks Paul was often misunderstood and was actually an advocate of sexual equality. Ronald Y. K. Fung, *The Epistle to the Galatians,* New International Commentary on the New Testament (Grand Rapids: Wm. B. Eerdmans Publishing Co., 1988), 175, argues, incorrectly in my opinion, that Paul was more interested in unity in the church than equality, thus being able in different letters to maintain contrary opinions about slavery and the role of women. It is more likely that his views changed over time.

6. See Hans Dieter Betz, *Galatians: A Commentary on Paul's Letter to the Churches in Galatia,* Hermenia (Philadelphia: Fortress Press, 1979), 190, 195.

7. Ben Witherington III, *Grace in Galatia: A Commentary on Paul's Letter to the Galatians* (Grand Rapids: Wm. B. Eerdmans Publishing Co., 1998), 165.

8. Thomas John Carlisle, "Room?" in *Beginning with Mary: Women of the Gospels in Portrait* (Grand Rapids: Wm. B. Eerdmans Publishing Co., 1986), 92.

9. Karen Jo Torjesen, *When Women Were Priests: Women's Leadership in the Early Church and the Scandal of Their Subordination in the Rise of Christianity* (San Francisco: HarperSanFrancisco, 1995), argues that women continued to be prominent leaders in the church for several centuries, even as bishops, and that the church eventually subordinated their power and tried to erase their service from the records.

10. Thomas John Carlise, "Beyond the Bounds," in *Beginning with Mary,* 100.

11. See Hans Conzelmann, *1 Corinthians: A Commentary on the First Epistle to the Corinthians,* Hermenia (Philadelphia: Fortress Press, 1975), 181–91.

12. For the background of this text and various interpretations of it, see Charles H. Talbert, *Reading Corinthians: A Literary and Theological Commentary on 1 and 2 Corinthians* (New

York: Crossroad, 1987), 66–72. See also Aurelia Fule, *A Biblical Inquiry: Should Women Keep Silence in the Churches?* (New York: Council on Women and the Church, UPCUSA, 1973).

13. Gordon D. Fee, *The First Epistle to the Corinthians* (Grand Rapids: Wm. B. Eerdmans Publishing Co., 1987), 708.

14. Bruggemann, *Genesis,* 42.

15. Feminist biblical scholars have added immeasurably to the correct understanding of the various ways in which women have been depicted in the Bible. See, among others, Johanna W. H. van Wijk-Bos, *Reformed and Feminist: A Challenge to the Church* (Louisville, Ky.: Westminster/John Knox Press, 1991), and Isabel Rogers' monograph, *Toward a Liberating Faith: A Primer on Feminist Theology* (Louisville, Ky.: Women's Ministries Program Area, PDS #72 700 00 002, 1999).

16. Barbara Hall, "Church in the World, Paul and Women," *Theology Today* 31 (1974): 55.

17. John Calvin, *The First Epistle of Paul the Apostle to the Corinthians,* ed. David W. Torrance and Thomas F. Torrance, trans. John W. Fraser (Grand Rapids: Wm. B. Eerdmans Publishing Co., 1960), 229.

18. Ibid., 232.

19. Ibid., 234.

20. Ibid., 306.

21. John Calvin, *The Second Epistle of Paul to the Corinthians, and the Epistles to Timothy, Titus, and Philemon,* ed. David W. Torrance and Thomas F. Torrance, trans. T. A. Smail (Grand Rapids: Wm. B. Eerdmans Publishing Co., 1964), 217.

22. Ibid., 217.

23. Lois A. Boyd and R. Douglas Brackenridge, "Presbyterian Women Ministers: A Historical Overview and Study of the Current Status of Women Pastors," in *The Pluralistic Vision: Presbyterians and Mainstream Protestant Education and Leadership,* ed. Milton J. Coalter, John M. Mulder, and Louis B. Weeks (Louisville, Ky.: Westminster/John Knox Press, 1992), 291.

24. This movement is carefully researched in the seminal work by Lois A. Boyd and R. Douglas Brackenridge, *Presbyterian Women in America: Two Centuries of a Quest for Status* (Westport, Conn.: Greenwood Press, 1983).

25. Barbara Brown Zikmund, "Ministry of Word and Sacrament: Women and Changing Understandings of Ordination," in *The Presbyterian Predicament: Six Perspectives,* ed. Milton J. Coalter, John M. Mulder, and Louis B. Weeks (Louisville, Ky.: Westminster/John Knox Press, 1990), 146.

26. For details of prior events, see Zikmund, "Ministry of Word and Sacrament," and Boyd and Brackenridge, *Presbyterian Women in America.* For a quick overview, see Smylie, *Brief History of the Presbyterians,* 104, 112–13, and Loetscher, *Brief History of the Presbyterians,* 99–100.

27. In *Selected Theological Statements,* 454–62.

28. The Kenyon case is discussed in some detail in Rogers, *Reading the Bible and the Confessions,* 104ff.

29. Fule, *A Biblical Inquiry,* 29. Provocative titles of articles in an evangelical magazine (no longer published) indicate the seriousness of the debate in some Christian communities: Dorothy L. Sayers, "Are Women Human?" *Eternity,* February 1974, 15–16; Nancy B. Barcus, "Jesus Doesn't Think I'm Dumb," *Eternity,* February 1974, 17–19.

30. The General Assembly papers mentioned in this paragraph are all found in *Selected Theological Statements.*

31. For a discussion of inclusive language, see Johnson, *Selected to Serve*, 54–58.

32. General Assembly statements on issues involving women's rights are summarized in *Presbyterian Social Witness Policy Compilation*, 323–42.

33. Stanton, *Woman's Bible*, 9.

34. See the excellent study by Kathi Kern, *Mrs. Stanton's Bible* (Ithaca, N.Y.: Cornell University Press, 2001).

35. Kern, *Mrs. Stanton's Bible*, 91.

36. For information about ACWC, see their webpage: www.pcusa.org/womensadvocacy/ACWC/index.htm.

37. Alex Smith, Jerry L. Van Marter, "Breaking the Silence: Chief of Women's Ministries Program Envisions New Global Women's Conference," *The News, Presbyterian Church (U.S.A.)*, August 31, 2001, 10–12.

38. See Patricia Golan, "Feminists in the Desert," *International Jerusalem Post*, August 17, 2001, 18–19.

39. See Glenda Daniels, "Gender Activists Slam Government," *Mail and Guardian* (Johannesburg), August 10–16, 2001, 8.

40. Stanton, *Woman's Bible*, 11.

CHAPTER 7: YOU HAVE NO EXCUSE WHEN YOU JUDGE OTHERS

1. The material in this chapter was first presented at a special meeting of the Presbytery of Albany on October 27, 1992. For exegetical studies of relevant passages, see recent biblical commentaries on pertinent texts. See especially Victor Paul Furnish, *The Moral Teaching of Paul, Selected Issues*, 2d ed. (Nashville: Abingdon Press, 1985). Bibliographic resources on this subject are enormous and cannot be listed in detail. An excellent sermon on the biblical texts was preached by H. Darrell Lance, professor of Old Testament interpretation, Colgate Rochester Divinity School, on February 16, 1992, and published as "Perfect Love Casts Out Fear," *Bulletin from the Hill* (Colgate Rochester Divinity School), 64, no. 1 (December 1992): 4, 7. See also the biblical study submitted by the original task force in the United Presbyterian Church in 1978 (later to become the minority report). For a recent book of essays from different perspectives, see Choon-Leong Seow, ed., *Homosexuality and Christian Community* (Louisville, Ky.: Westminster John Knox Press, 1996).

2. Furnish, *Moral Teaching of Paul*, 80.

3. "Homosexuality: Neither Sin nor Sickness," *Trends* (July-August 1973), ed. by Dennis E. Shoemaker and Florence V. Bryant. Published by Geneva Press, the magazine was discontinued some time thereafter.

4. *Presbyterian Social Witness Policy Compilation*, 395–96.

5. For reviews of the debates around Amendment B and Amendment A, see articles in the *Presbyterian Outlook*, January 5–12, 1998, and January 26, 1998.

6. I am indebted to Daniel Patte for his insights into the significance of this debate. See *The Challenge of Discipleship: A Critical Study of the Sermon on the Mount as Scripture* (Harrisburg, Pa.: Trinity Press International, 1999), 8–10.

7. See Leslie Weatherhead, "Did Jesus Repudiate the Old Testament?" in *When the Lamp Flickers* (London: Hodder & Stoughton, 1948).

8. J. Andrew Overman, *Matthew's Gospel and Formative Judaism* (Philadelphia: Fortress Press, 1990), 112.

9. L. Michael White, "Crisis Management and Boundary Location: The Social Location of the Matthean Community," in *Social History of the Matthean Community: Cross-Disciplinary Approaches*, ed. David L. Balch (Philadelphia: Fortress Press, 1991), 224.

10. Wayne Meeks, *The First Urban Christians: The Social World of the Apostle Paul* (New Haven, Conn.: Yale University Press, 1983), 84–107.

11. Robert Frost, "Mending Wall," in *Selected Poems of Robert Frost* (New York: Holt, Rinehart & Winston, 1963), 23–24.

CHAPTER 8: HE IS OUR PEACE

1. Best, *Ephesians,* 251.

2. See Johnson, *Galatians and Ephesians,* 115–17.

3. Three sources stand out: The Confession of 1967, "Peacemaking: The Believers' Calling" (UPCUSA, 1980, DMS, OGA-88-047), and "Just Peacemaking and the Call for International Intervention for Humanitarian Rescue" (PC(U.S.A.), 1998) in *Selected Theological Statements,* 324–52.

4. John T. McNeill, "Editor's Introduction," in *On God and Political Duty* (Indianapolis: Bobbs-Merrill Co., 1956), vii–xxv.

5. See Louis Weeks, "Faith and Political Action in American Presbyterianism, 1776–1918," in *Reformed Faith and Politics: Essays Prepared for the Advisory Council on Church and Society of the UPCUSA,* ed. Ronald H. Stone (Washington, D.C.: University Press of America, 1983), 101.

6. "Peacemaking: The Believers' Calling," 4.

7. "Just Peacemaking and the Call," 351.

8. Earl S. Johnson Jr., "He Is Our Peace," *Presbyterian Outlook,* October 22, 2001, 21.

Bibliography

Achtemeier, Paul J., ed. *Harper's Bible Dictionary*. San Francisco: Harper & Row, 1985.

Adams, John H. "Evangelicals Rally behind Confessing Church Movement." *Presbyterian Layman,* April 2001, 1–2.

Bailey, Lloyd R. *Genesis, Creation, and Creationism*. Mahwah, N.J.: Paulist Press, 1993.

Barcus, Nancy B. "Jesus Doesn't Think I'm Dumb." *Eternity,* February 1974, 17–19.

Bax, Douglas. "The Bible and Apartheid 2." In *Apartheid Is a Heresy,* edited by John W. DeGrucy and Charles Villa-Vincencio. Grand Rapids: Wm. B. Eerdmans Publishing Co., 1987.

Best, Ernest. *The Letter of Paul to the Romans*. Cambridge Bible Commentary of the New English Bible. Cambridge: Cambridge University Press, 1967.

Betz, Hans Dieter. *Galatians: A Commentary on Paul's Letter to the Churches in Galatia*. Hermenia. Philadelphia: Fortress Press, 1979.

Boesak, Allan A. "What Belongs to Caesar? Once Again Romans 13." In *When Prayer Makes News*. Edited by Allan A. Boesak and Charles Villa-Vincencio. Philadelphia: Westminster Press, 1986, 138–56.

Borg, Marcus J. *Jesus in Contemporary Scholarship*. Valley Forge, Pa.: Trinity Press International, 1994.

———. *Reading the Bible Again for the First Time: Taking the Bible Seriously but Not Literally*. San Francisco: HarperSanFrancisco, 2001.

Boswell, James O., III. *Slavery, Segregation, and Scripture*. Grand Rapids: Wm. B. Eerdmans Publishing Co., 1964.

Boyd, Lois A., and R. Douglas Brackenridge. *Presbyterian Women in America: Two Centuries of a Quest for Status*. A Publication of the Presbyterian Historical Society. Westport, Conn.: Greenwood Press, 1983.

———. "Presbyterian Women Ministers: A Historical Overview and Study of the Current Status of Women Pastors." In *The Pluralistic Vision: Presbyterians and Mainstream Protestant Education and Leadership,* edited by Milton J. Coalter, John M. Mulder, and Louis B. Weeks. Louisville, Ky.: Westminster/John Knox Press, 1992, 289–307.

Bristow, John Temple. *What Paul Really Said about Women: An Apostle's Liberating Views on Equality in Marriage, Leadership, and Love*. San Francisco: Harper & Row, 1988.

Brueggemann, Walter. "Exodus." In *The New Interpreter's Bible,* vol. 1. Nashville: Abingdon Press, 1999.

———. *Genesis*. Interpretation: A Bible Commentary for Teaching and Preaching. Atlanta: John Knox Press, 1982.

Building Community among Strangers: A Report on Racism, Social Class Division, Sex-Based Injustices, Religious Intolerance and Conflict, Approved by the 211th General Assembly (1999). Louisville, Ky.: Office of the General Assembly Presbyterian Church (U.S.A.), PDS # OGA-99-028, 1999.

Burgess, John P. ed., *In Whose Image? Faith, Science, and the New Genetics*. Louisville, Ky.: Geneva Press, 1998.

Busch, Eberhard. *Karl Barth: His Life from Letters and Autobiographical Texts*. Translated by John Bowden. Philadelphia: Fortress Press, 1976.

Calvin, John. "Articles concerning Predestination." In *Calvin: Theological Treatises*. Library of Christian Classics. Translated by J. K. S. Reid. Philadelphia: The Westminster Press, 1954, 178–80.

———. *The First Epistle of Paul to the Corinthians*. Translated by John W. Fraser. Edited by David W. Torrance and Thomas F. Torrance. Grand Rapids: Wm. B. Eerdmans Publishing Co., 1960.

———. *Institutes of the Christian Religion*. Edited by John T. McNeill. Translated by Ford Lewis Battles. Philadelphia: Westminster Press, 1960.

———. *The Second Epistle of Paul to the Corinthians, and the Epistles to Timothy, Titus, and Philemon*. Translated by T. A. Smail. Edited by David W. Torrance and Thomas F. Torrance. Grand Rapids: Wm. B. Eerdmans Publishing Co., 1964.

Carlisle, Thomas John. *Beginning with Mary: Women of the Gospels in Portrait*. Grand Rapids: Wm. B. Eerdmans Publishing Co., 1986.

Chirichigno, Gregory C. *Debt-Slavery in Israel and the Ancient Near East*. Journal for the Study of the Old Testament Supplement Series 141. Sheffield: Sheffield Academic Press, 1993.

Clifford, Richard J. *Creation Accounts in the Ancient Near East and in the Bible*. Catholic Biblical Quarterly Monograph Series 24. Washington, D.C.: Catholic Biblical Association, 1994.

Combes, I. A. H. *The Metaphor of Slavery in the Writings of the Early Church: From the New Testament to the Beginning of the Fifth Century*. Journal for the Study of the New Testament Supplement Series 156. Sheffield: Sheffield Academic Press, 1998.

"The Confessional Nature of the Church." General Assembly Minutes 1986. In *Selected Theological Statements of the Presbyterian Church (U.S.A.) General Assemblies (1956–1998)*. Louisville, Ky.: Office of Theology and Worship, Congregational Ministries Division Presbyterian Church (U.S.A.), 1998, 89–115.

"A Conversation with Bill McKibben." *Alive Now!* July/August 2000, 28–33.

Conzelmann, Hans. *1 Corinthians: A Commentary on the First Epistle to the Corinthians*. Hermenia. Philadelphia: Fortress Press, 1975.

Crouch, Archie. "Racial-Ethnic Ministry Policies: An Historical Overview." *Journal of Presbyterian History* 57 (1979): 272–313.

Daniels, Glenda. "Gender Activists Slam Government." *Johannesburg Mail and Guardian*, August 10–16, 2001, 8.

A Digest of the General Assembly Proceedings, Presbyterian Church U.S., 1861–1944, Authorized by the General Assembly. Richmond: Presbyterian Committee on Publication, 1945.

Dodd, C. H. *The Epistle of Paul to the Romans*. London and Glasgow: Fontana Books, 1963.

Eberts, Harry W., Jr. *We Believe: A Study of the Book of Confessions for Church Officers*. Philadelphia: Geneva Press, 1987.

Effective Christian Education: A National Study of Protestant Congregations. A Research Project of the Search Institute. Minneapolis: The Search Institute, 1990.

Fee, Gordon D. *The First Epistle to the Corinthians.* Grand Rapids: Wm. B. Eerdmans Publishing Co., 1987.

Fitzmyer, Joseph A. "New Testament Kyrios and Maranatha and Their Aramaic Background." In *To Advance the Gospel: New Testament Studies.* New York: Crossroad, 1981.

———. *Romans: A New Translation with Introduction and Commentary.* Anchor Bible. New York: Doubleday, 1993.

Fox, Everett. *The Five Books of Moses: Genesis, Exodus, Leviticus, Numbers, and Deuteronomy. A New Translation with Introduction, Commentary, and Notes.* New York: Schocken Books, 1995.

Fretheim, Terence E. "The Book of Genesis." In *New Interpreter's Bible,* vol. 1. Nashville: Abingdon Press, 1994.

Frost, Robert. "Mending Wall." In *Selected Poems of Robert Frost.* New York: Holt, Rinehart & Winston, 1963, 23–24.

Fule, Aurelia. *A Biblical Inquiry: Should Women Keep Silence in the Churches?* New York: Council on Women and the Church, UPCUSA, 1973.

Fuller, R. H. "Lord." In *Harper's Bible Dictionary,* edited by Paul J. Achtemeier. San Francisco: Harper & Row, 1985

Fung, Ronald Y. K. *The Epistle to the Galatians.* New International Commentary on the New Testament. Grand Rapids: Wm. B. Eerdmans Publishing Co., 1988.

Furnish, Victor Paul. *The Moral Teaching of Paul: Selected Issues.* 2nd ed. Nashville: Abingdon Press, 1985.

"GAC Affirms Lordship of Christ, Defends 'Open Dialogue' in Conferences." *The News, Presbyterian Church (U.S.A.),* March 9, 2001, 5–6.

Golan, Patricia. "Feminists in the Desert." *International Jerusalem Post,* August 17, 2001, 18–19.

Hall, Barbara. "Church in the World, Paul and Women." *Theology Today* 31 (1974): 50–55.

Handbook for Ecumenical and Interfaith Relations. Louisville, Ky.: Global Mission Ministry Unit, Office of Ecumenical and Interfaith Relations, 1992.

Harvey, Van A. *A Handbook of Theological Terms.* New York: Macmillan, 1964.

Hengel, Martin. *Studies in Early Christianity.* Edinburgh: T. & T. Clark, 1995.

Herzog, William R., II. *Jesus, Justice, and the Reign of God: A Ministry of Liberation.* Louisville, Ky.: Westminster John Knox Press, 2000.

Hope for a Global Future: Toward Just and Sustainable Human Development. Approved by the 208th General Assembly (1996) Presbyterian Church (U.S.A.). Louisville, Ky.: Presbyterian Distribution Service, 1996.

Horsley, Richard A., ed. *Paul and Empire: Religion and Power in Roman Imperial Society.* Harrisburg, Pa.: Trinity Press International, 1997.

Jewett, Robert. *Paul the Apostle to America: Cultural Trends and Pauline Scholarship.* Louisville, Ky.: Westminster John Knox Press, 1994.

Johnson, Earl and Elinore Johnson. *The History of First Presbyterian Church, Williamson, New York, 1816–2000.* Williamson, N.Y.: Frostbytes Computer Services, 2000.

Johnson, Earl S., Jr. *Galatians and Ephesians.* Basic Bible Commentary. Nashville: Abingdon Press, 1994.

———. "He Is Our Peace." *Presbyterian Outlook,* October 22, 2001, 21.

———. *James; First and Second Peter; First, Second, and Third John; and Jude.* Basic Bible Commentary. Nashville: Abingdon Press, 1994.

———. "Mark 5:1–20: The Other Side." *Irish Biblical Studies* 20 (1998): 50–74.

———. "Mark 15.39 and the So-Called Confession of the Roman Centurion." *Biblica* 81 (2000): 406–13.

————. *Selected to Serve: A Guide for Church Officers.* Louisville, Ky.: Geneva Press, 2000.

Johnson, William Stacey. "Confessional Wellness and Its Challenge." *Presbyterian Outlook,* May 14, 2001, 1, 8.

————. "Equally Yoked." *Presbyterian Outlook,* May 28, 2001, 11.

The Kairos Document: Challenge to the Church: A Theological Comment on the Political Crisis in South Africa. Grand Rapids: Wm. B. Eerdmans Publishing Co., 1986.

Katzin, Donna. "Economic Strategies: An Evolving Prophetic Partnership between South African and U.S. Churches." In *A Long Struggle: The Involvement of the World Council of Churches in South Africa,* edited by Pauline Webb. Geneva: WCC Publications, 1994.

Keeping and Healing the Creation. Louisville, Ky.: Committee on Social Witness Policy, Presbyterian Church (U.S.A.), 1989.

Kern, Kathi. *Mrs. Stanton's Bible.* Ithaca, N.Y.: Cornell University Press, 2001.

Kluger, Jeffrey. "Global Warming: A Climate for Despair." *Time,* April 9, 2001, 30–36.

Lance, Darrel H. "Perfect Love Casts Out Fear." *Bulletin from the Hill* (Colgate Rochester Divinity School). December 1992, 4–7.

Leakey, Richard. "Extinctions Past and Present." *Time,* Spring 2000, special ed., *Earth Day 2000,* 35.

Leith, John. *Basic Christian Doctrines.* Louisville, Ky.: Westminster/John Knox Press, 1993.

Linden, Eugene. "State of the Planet: Condition Critical." *Time,* Spring 2000, special ed., *Earth Day 2000,* 18–24.

Lindsay, Vachel. "The Unpardonable Sin." In *Chapters into Verse: Poetry in English Inspired by the Bible.* Vol. 2, *Gospels to Revelation,* edited by Robert Atwan and Laurance Wieder. Oxford and New York: Oxford University Press, 1993, 93.

Loetscher, Lefferts A. *A Brief History of the Presbyterians.* Revised and enlarged. Philadelphia: Westminster Press, 1958.

Longenecker, Richard D. *Galatians.* Word Biblical Commentary. Dallas: Word, 1990.

Longfield, Bradley J. *The Presbyterian Controversy: Fundamentalists, Modernists, and Moderates.* New York: Oxford University Press, 1991.

Loubser, J. A. *A Critical Review of Racial Theology in South Africa: The Apartheid Bible.* Lewiston, N.Y.: Edwin Mellen Press, 1987.

Luther, Martin. *A Commentary on St. Paul's Epistle to the Galatians.* Translated by Phillip S. Watson. London: James Clarke and Co., 1961.

————. *Martin Luther: Selections from His Writings.* Translated by John Dillenberger. Garden City, N.Y.: Anchor Books, 1961.

Mandela, Nelson. *The Long Walk to Freedom.* Boston: Little, Brown & Co., 1994.

Marshall, I. Howard. *The Origins of New Testament Christology.* Updated ed. Downers Grove, Ill.: InterVarsity Press, 1990.

Matera, Frank J. *New Testament Christology.* Louisville, Ky.: Westminster John Knox Press, 1999.

McCarter, P. Kyle. "Exodus." In *Harper's Bible Commentary,* edited by James L. Mays. San Francisco: Harper & Row, 1988.

McDaniel, Carl N., and John M. Gowdy. *Paradise for Sale: A Parable of Nature.* Berkeley, Calif.: University of California Press, 2000.

McFague, Sallie. *The Body of God: An Ecological Theology.* Minneapolis: Fortress Press, 1994.

McKelway, A. J. "Reflections on Dirk Ficca's Speech." *Presbyterian Outlook,* April 16, 2001, 6–7.

McKenzie, Steven L. *All God's Children: A Biblical Critique of Racism.* Louisville, Ky.: Westminster John Knox Press, 1997.

McKibben, Bill. "Climate Change and the Unraveling of Creation." *Christian Century,* December 8, 1999, 1197.

McKim, Lindajo H. *The Presbyterian Hymnal Companion.* Louisville, Ky.: Westminster/John Knox Press, 1993.

McNeill, John T, ed. *John Calvin: On God and Political Duty.* Indianapolis: Bobbs-Merrill Co., 1956.

Meeks, Wayne. *The First Urban Christians: The Social World of the Apostle Paul.* New Haven, Conn.: Yale University Press, 1983.

Migliore, Daniel L. "The Ecological Crisis and the Doctrine of Creation." *Princeton Theological Seminary Bulletin* 12, no. 3 (1991): 266–82.

Moltmann, Jürgen. *Jesus Christ for Today's World.* Translated by Margaret Kohl. Minneapolis: Fortress Press, 1994.

"The Nature of Revelation in Christian Tradition from a Reformed Perspective." In *Selected Theological Statements of the Presbyterian Church (U.S.A.) General Assemblies (1956–1998).* Louisville, Ky.: Theology and Worship, Christian Faith and Life, Congregational Ministries Division, 1998.

The Nature of the Church and the Practice of Governance, Approved by the 205th General Assembly (1993) Presbyterian Church (U.S.A.). Louisville, Ky.: Office of the General Assembly, 1993.

Nichols, James Hastings. *Presbyterianism in New York State: A History of the Synod and Its Predecessors.* Philadelphia: Westminster Press, 1963.

Oberman, Heiko A. *Luther: Man between God and the Devil.* New Haven, Conn.: Yale University Press, 1989.

O'Connell, Kevin G. "Exodus," In *Harper's Bible Dictionary,* edited by Paul J. Achtemeier. San Francisco: Harper & Row, 1985.

Overman, J. Andrew. *Matthew's Gospel and Formative Judaism.* Philadelphia: Fortress Press, 1990.

Parker, Harold M., Jr. *The United Synod of the South: The Southern New School Presbyterian Church.* A Publication of the Presbyterian Historical Society. New York: Greenwood Press, 1988.

Patte, Daniel. *The Challenge of Discipleship: A Critical Study of the Sermon on the Mount as Scripture.* Harrisburg, Pa.: Trinity Press International, 1999.

———. *The Gospel according to Matthew: A Structural Commentary on Matthew's Gospel.* Valley Forge, Pa.: Trinity Press International, 1987.

Polk, Peggy. "Catholic, Lutheran, and Reformed Churches Discuss Indulgences." Religion News Service, reported by Presbyterian News Service, February 26, 2001, 01078.

———. "Vatican Declares Only the Roman Catholic Church Brings Salvation." Religion News Service, reported by Presbyterian News Service, September 7, 2000, 00321.

The Presbyterian Hymnal. Louisville, Ky.: Westminster/John Knox Press, 1990.

Presbyterian Social Witness Policy Compilation, Presbyterian Church (U.S.A.) and Its Antecedents, Presbyterian Church in the U.S. and the United Presbyterian Church in the U.S.A. 1946–1999. Louisville, Ky.: Office of the General Assembly: Advisory Committee on Social Witness Policy of the General Assembly, 2000.

"Presbyterian Theology, Policy, and Witness regarding South Africa." In *Minutes of the General Assembly,* Part I, *Journal,* New York and Atlanta: Office of the General Assembly, 1985.

Presbyterian Understanding and Use of the Holy Scriptures: Position Statement Adopted by the General Assembly (1983) of the Presbyterian Church in the United States of America and *Biblical Authority and Interpretation: A Resource Document Received by the 194th General Assembly (1982) of the United Presbyterian Church in the United States of America*. Louisville, Ky.: Office of Theology and Worship, Presbyterian Church (U.S.A.), 1998, PDS #70420–98-006.

Records of the Presbyterian Church in the United States of America, Embracing the Minutes of the General Presbytery and the General Synod, 1706–1788. Philadelphia: Presbyterian Board of Publication and Sabbath-School Work, 1904. Reprint, New York: Arno Press, 1969.

Restoring Creation for Ecology and Justice. A Report Adopted by the 202nd General Assembly (1990) Presbyterian Church (U.S.A.). Louisville, Ky.: Office of the General Assembly, 1990.

Rigby, Cynthia L. "Jesus Is the Way: Presbyterian Theology Affirms the Uniqueness of Christ." *Presbyterians Today*, April 2001, 15–17.

Rogers, Isabel. *Toward a Liberating Faith: A Primer on Feminist Theology*. Louisville, Ky.: Women's Ministries Program Area, PDS #72 700 00 002, 1999.

Rogers, Jack. *Presbyterian Creeds*. Louisville, Ky.: Westminster/John Knox Press, 1991.

———. *Reading the Bible and the Confessions: The Presbyterian Way*. Louisville, Ky.: Geneva Press, 1999.

Rogers, Jack B., and Donald K. McKim. "Pluralism and Policy in Presbyterian Views of Scripture." In *The Confessional Mosaic: Presbyterians and Twentieth-Century Theology*, edited by Milton J. Coalter, John M. Mulder, and Louis B. Weeks. Louisville, Ky.: Westminster/John Knox Press, 1990.

Rolston, Holmes, III. "The Bible and Ecology." *Interpretation*, January 1996, 16–27.

Rosenblatt, Roger. "Why Protecting the Environment Means Saving Ourselves All the Days of the Earth." *Time*, Spring 2000, special ed., *Earth Day 2000*, 9–15.

Sayers, Dorothy L. "Are Women Human?" *Eternity*, February 1974, 15–16.

Scanlon, Leslie. "Montreat Church to File Complaint against GAC." *Presbyterian Outlook*, June 11, 2001, 3.

Seow, Choon-Leong, ed. *Homosexuality and Christian Community*. Louisville, Ky.: Westminster John Knox Press, 1996.

Selected Theological Statements of the Presbyterian Church (U.S.A.) General Assemblies. Louisville, Ky.: Presbyterian Church (U.S.A.), 1998.

Shoemaker, Dennis E., and Florence V. Bryant, eds., "Homosexuality: Neither Sin nor Sickness." *Trends*, vol. 5, no. 6, July-August 1973.

Smart, James. *The Strange Silence of the Bible in the Church: A Study in Hermeneutics*. Philadelphia: Westminster Press, 1970.

Smith, Alexa, and Jerry L. Van Marter. "Breaking the Silence: Chief of Women's Ministries Program Envisions New Global Women's Conference." *The News, Presbyterian Church (U.S.A.)*, August 31, 2001, 10–12.

Smylie, James H. *A Brief History of the Presbyterians*. Louisville, Ky.: Geneva Press, 1996.

Stanton, Elizabeth Cady. *Eighty Years and More, Reminiscences 1815–1897*. 1898. Reprint, Boston: Northeastern University Press, 1993.

———. *The Woman's Bible*. 1898. Reprint, Amherst, N.Y.: Prometheus Books, 1999.

Stanton, Elizabeth Cady, and Susan B. Anthony. *The History of Woman Suffrage*, vol. 3. 1886. Reprint, Manchester, N.H.: Ayer Company, 1979.

Stimpson, Eva. "Don't Dodge the Jesus Debate." *Presbyterians Today*, January-February 2001, 2.

Talbert, Charles H. *Reading Corinthians: A Literary and Theological Commentary on 1 and 2 Corinthians*. New York: Crossroad, 1987.

Tamez, Elsa. *The Amnesty of Grace: Justification by Faith from a Latin American Perspective.* Translated by Sharon H. Ringe. Nashville: Abingdon Press, 1993.

———. *The Scandalous Message of James: Faith without Works Is Dead.* Translated by John Eagleson. New York: Crossroad, 1992.

"Three Conservative Credos Fuel Confessing 'Movement,'" *The News, Presbyterian Church (U.S.A.),* April 27, 2001, 5.

Torjesen, Karen Jo. *When Women Were Priests: Women's Leadership in the Early Church and the Scandal of Their Subordination in the Rise of Christianity.* San Francisco: HarperSanFrancisco, 1995.

Tuckett, Christopher. *Christology and the New Testament: Jesus and His Earliest Followers.* Louisville, Ky.: Westminster John Knox Press, 2001.

"Turn to the Living God: A Call to Evangelism in Christ's Way" (203rd General Assembly, 1991). In *Selected Theological Statements, General Assemblies (1956–1998).* Louisville, Ky.: Theology and Worship, Christian Faith and Life, Congregational Ministries Division, 1998.

Tutu, Desmond. "Address to Deacons." In *Hope and Suffering: Sermons and Speeches.* Compiled by Mothobi Mutloatse. Edited by John Webster. Grand Rapids: Wm. B. Eerdmans Publishing Co., 1984.

———. *The Rainbow People of God: The Making of a Peaceful Revolution.* Edited by John Allen. New York: Doubleday, 1994.

Using the Bible: A Guided Study of Presbyterian Statements on Biblical Authority and Interpretation. Louisville, Ky.: Theology and Worship Ministry Unit, Presbyterian Church (U.S.A.), 1993, DMS #277-92-101.

Van Marter, Jerry L. "Presbyterians Travel to the Vatican in Search of Unity with Roman Catholics." Presbyterian News Service, March 27, 2001, 01106.

Villa-Vincencio, Charles. *The Theology of Apartheid.* Cape Town: Methodist Publishing House, 1977.

———, ed. *On Reading Karl Barth in South Africa.* Grand Rapids: Wm. B. Eerdmans Publishing Co., 1988.

Vorster, Willem. "The Bible and Apartheid 1." In *Apartheid Is a Heresy,* edited by John W. DeGrucy and Charles Villa-Vincencio. Grand Rapids: Wm. B. Eerdmans Publishing Co., 1987.

Weatherhead, Leslie. "Did Jesus Repudiate the Old Testament?" In *When the Lamp Flickers.* London: Hodder & Stoughton, 1948, 24–37.

———. *The Will of God.* London: Epworth Press, 1944.

Webb, Pauline, ed. *A. Long Struggle: The Involvement of the World Council of Churches in South Africa.* Geneva: WCC Publications, 1994.

Wedderburn, A. J. *The Reasons for Romans.* Minneapolis: Fortress Press, 1991.

Weeks, Louis. "Faith and Political Action in American Presbyterianism, 1776–1918." In *Reformed Faith and Politics: Essays Prepared for the Advisory Council on Church and Society of the UPCUSA.* Edited by Ronald H. Stone. Washington, D.C.: University Press of America, 1983, 110–19.

Weld, Theodore Dwight. *The Bible against Slavery, or An Inquiry into the Genius of the Teachings of the Mosaic System, and the Teachings of the Old Testament on the Subject of Human Rights* (1864). Republished, Detroit: Negro History Press, 1970.

Wenham, Gordon J. *Genesis 1–15.* Word Biblical Commentary. Waco, Tex.: Word, 1987.

White, L. Michael. "Crisis Management and Boundary Location: The Social Location of the Matthean Community." In *Social History of the Matthean Community: Cross-Disciplinary Approaches,* edited by David L. Balch. Philadelphia: Fortress Press, 1991, 211–47.

White, Vera K. *Healing and Defending God's Creation: Hands On! Practical Ideas for Congregations,* vol. 2. Louisville, Ky.: Presbyterian Church (U.S.A.), DMS #259-93-939.

Wijk-Bos, Johanna W. H. van. *Reformed and Feminist: A Challenge to the Church.* Louisville, Ky.: Westminster/John Knox Press, 1991.

Witherington, Ben, III. *Grace in Galatia: A Commentary on Paul's Letter to the Galatians.* Grand Rapids: Wm. B. Eerdmans Publishing Co., 1998.

Zikmund, Barbara Brown. "Ministry of Word and Sacrament: Women and Changing Understandings of Ordination." In *The Presbyterian Predicament: Six Perspectives,* edited by Milton J. Coalter, John M. Mulder, and Louis B. Weeks. Louisville, Ky.: Westminster/John Knox Press, 1990, 134–58.

Index of Scriptural References

Index of *Book of Order* References

Index of *Book of Confessions* References

Auhor Index

Subject Index